Stramullion

a Scottish-based feminist publishing collective

INCEST
Fact and Myth

Sarah Nelson

First published in 1982, 2nd revised edition 1987 by
Stramullion Co-operative Limited
11a Forth Street, Edinburgh, EH1 3LE

Reprinted 1988

British Library Cataloguing in Publication Data
Nelson, Sarah
Incest : fact and myth.—2nd ed., rev
and updated
1. Incest   2. Fathers and daughters
I. Title
306.7'77 HQ71

ISBN 0 907343 06 6

Cartoons by Dianne Barry
Cover design by Rebecca and Sue Innes

Photoset and printed in Great Britain by
Redwood Burn Limited, Trowbridge, Wiltshire

Contents

Preface

It is four years since the first edition of this book was published. During that time child sexual abuse in general, and incestuous abuse in particular, have become more widely acknowledged and discussed as major social problems in Britain. New writing and research from the British Isles and United States have been very helpful to many others besides myself, while conferences and discussions have given people mutual support as well as much-needed information. They have also built many bridges between professional workers and others.

The major development has been the growth of incest survivor groups whose individual and collective courage cannot be overstated. Their determination to speak out has brought some shift in professional attitudes away from overt victim-blame, but many myths of incest still persist. While the need to repair the damage caused by incestuous abuse is more widely recognised there is still little in the way of co-ordinated intervention or serious efforts at prevention, which must surely be the priority in future.

I should like to thank everyone who has helped me put together both editions of this book, and stress that any errors are my own. I am especially grateful to Emily Driver, Kathy Kerr, Audrey Middleton, Rasjidah St John, Clodagh Corcoran and Anne O'Donnell, and also thank for their encouragement all the women and men who urged me to bring out a second edition. The biggest debt is to Noreen Winchester whose experience caused me to research and write this book. Noreen wishes to build a new life and readers, researchers and journalists are asked to respect her privacy.

The use of the term 'survivor' is a recent development. In the words of Scottish Action against Incest:

> The women involved in survivors groups have a great distaste for the term 'victim of incest'. Because the function of a

victim is to give in. Because a victim is one who has been struck down and who accepts herself as a victim, who by staying down can still be humiliated and will offer no protest.

A survivor of incest, on the other hand, is someone who has protested and fought, and signals that she will not tolerate further abuse, be it from others or from herself through self-oppression ... to be a survivor is the victorious conclusion.

Many writers, researchers and therapists have not intended this unsympathetic connotation by the term 'victim': that is accepted in this book, but perhaps rethinking on its implications is now overdue.

Likewise many girls and women, abused at present or in the past, have not yet found a way of surviving that frees them from oppression or self-oppression. To enable them to reach the 'victorious conclusion', the least duty the rest of society has is to hear what they are saying, and to act upon it.

Introduction

Incest is distasteful, even shocking, to most people: but at least it has nothing to do with nasty things like rape, or child molesting, or the sexual abuse of women. The idea is absurd. For everyone knows incest is a quaint custom indulged in by simple people who live in the hills, especially the Appalachian mountains. Or the west of Ireland, or the Fens, or Melanesia.

Alternatively, it happens not to isolated but to overcrowded people like the lower classes of squalid slums in Glasgow, Chicago or places like that. But not to worry too much, because everyone knows it's a tiny problem. Incest, as one team of experts assures us, 'is not a common phenomenon among civilised people'. Drunks and deviants and subcultures may do it, but never families like ours. Enlightened groups, like the National Council for Civil Liberties, think there shouldn't even be a crime of incest: what right have we to impose our sexual mores on those who have freely chosen different loving relationships from our own?

Unfortunately there are a few problems about these popular views.

In more than 90 per cent of incest cases, one of the 'consenting adults' is a girl child. Her average age when she 'agrees' to begin the relationship is eight or nine. The other consenting adult is a grown man, who is usually her father.

Incestuous fathers are not confined to crofters and lower class alcoholics. They include judges, professors, doctors, ministers and policemen.

They often use violence, threats, blackmail or social isolation to bind their 'loving' relationships. One girl's account of such a relationship described by Stucker:

> My dad said that if I told my mother he would kill me ... it hurt, I remember crying; I didn't understand what he was doing ... most of the time I would just feel powerless and cry. I'd just

lie there and hope it would hurry and be over. At night when he came in, I would crawl really close to the wall ... I actually believed (that if I did) he wouldn't be able to touch me. But he always got me.

Many girls get pregnant, often before they even understand about sex and conception. Incest can cause vaginal lesions, internal bleeding, serious venereal disease, bone dislocation and (in young children) even death. Research has found that psychological damage includes chronic depression, suicide attempts, neurosis, revulsion against sex, and self-disgust. Abused girls feature heavily among those who take up prostitution. In the words of Henry Kempe, an authority on child abuse:

Incest victims see themselves as defenceless, worthless, guilty and threatened from all sides, particularly by the father and mother who would be expected to be their protectors.

The final problem is that incest is not unusual. For many reasons, the vast majority of cases never come to light at all: we see only the tip of the iceberg.

Given the youth of many of the abused children and the damage that is done, we would expect the fiercest reaction from society against adults who commit incest. For no one excites more hostility than the man who 'interferes' with children. The popular Press rages against these 'beasts': many people regard them as the worst of all criminals. Such offenders must spend their whole jail term in solitary confinement, to protect them from other prisoners. Declared members of Paedophile Information Exchange (PIE) have lost their jobs and suffered physical and verbal abuse, including death threats. Public campaigns are also waged against the commercial exploitation of children in sex films and magazines.

Yet we find no such public reaction to incest offenders: indeed they are rarely even talked about. Why this stark inconsistency?

One reason is that most people are unaware of facts that might provoke condemnation, or even acknowledgement that the problem exists. For incest is still a taboo subject, even in our so-called permissive society. Those who know it happens through experience are too ashamed or afraid to speak out, while the majority avoid looking for evidence to challenge their belief that it is a tiny problem.

Newspapers and magazines, who do not shrink from treating even rape as a source of titillation, seem to agree with the public

that incest is too distasteful to talk about. English news editors have been heard to say it is not something that people want to read about at the breakfast-table or read about in a family news-paper.

The same feelings of revulsion (say Kempe and Kempe) 'have caused professionals to shy away from the problem of sexual abuse and to underestimate its severity and extent'. Many admit they find the subject abhorrent and difficult to discuss: they also admit they simply do not know what to do when confronted with cases of incest.

Another reason for the lack of condemnation is that many re-searchers, and professionals who treat incestuous families, have not felt seriously concerned about such behaviour. Nor have they seen it as an issue of child abuse. Instead there has been a strong tendency to treat incest as an interesting curiosity, or to shift blame from the adult offender to the child and her mother. Much of the literature implies that incestuous men are not really crimi-nals, and that the children invited, enjoyed or accepted their sexual experiences.

Thus we have an ironic situation. The people who condemn incest cannot believe it happens much; they take no action and have no influence. Those who know it happens through their direct contact with families, those who influence policy directly, are the very people who make excuses for incest. The result of inaction from one group, and justification from the other, has been that in our society neither incest offenders nor their victims have been taken seriously.

In the following pages I aim to give people more information about facts and figures; to question various myths that underpin current professional practice; and to put forward alternative interpretations of incest. Though all forms of incest are discussed, I have concentrated on the most common form, the relationships between daughters and their fathers or stepfathers.

I contend that far from being small-scale and unusual incest is widespread; that in the great majority of cases we cannot talk of meaningful consent by the child; that incest causes serious physical and psychological harm and is a significant cause of adult mental illness, and that the cause of incest is not complex and mysterious. Instead, it is a simple and straightforward form of sexual abuse and exploitation of female children by adult men, for the selfish purpose of sexual gratification.

I believe that professional attitudes to incest have not been neutral but heavily biased and ill-founded. They have caused and perpetuated much suffering among families, and increased the distress among incest survivors.

The same traditional views about the nuclear family and male and female sexuality which have encouraged adult men into incest, have also influenced professional practice towards incestuous families. The patriarchal tradition holds that the man as head of the household has the right to exert authority, and expect his womenfolk to serve his needs. Traditional attitudes encourage the belief that we should not interfere with what people do within their own four walls, and that families should be kept together, whatever the cost. They also encourage the belief that men are naturally aggressive, have high sexual needs, and cannot be expected to endure abstinence for long. In contrast, women really ask for sexual abuse, collude in it, enjoy it, or simply invent it.

Just as expert writing about incest has much in common with expert writing on wife-beating and rape, so the crime of incest has many links with general sex crimes, and with other forms of violence within the family. Incest is related to a general pattern of male sexual assaults like rape. Much of this is culturally sanctioned or not taken seriously by society, and most assaults are never reported. Incest is also a product of the family structure: but the clue lies in normal family values, not deviant ones. Like wife-beating, incest is likely to happen when traditional beliefs about the roles of husband, wife and daughter are taken to extremes: when the family members are seen as the husband's property, and sex is among the services they are expected to provide.

Some readers will no doubt feel these arguments are just anti-men.

But there is no question of implying that 'all men are guilty'. It is because most men would not think of sexually abusing their daughters that they find it so hard to face the possibility that some men do so. But it is only when both men and women admit that possibility that they can begin to tackle the problem. Facing up to reality may be threatening, unpleasant or unpalatable, but it may actually do something to help those who are abused. Wallowing in self-righteous indignation may be reassuring, but it is no help to anybody. It merely ensures that existing levels of abuse will continue.

If people feel these arguments are just anti-family, they must ask themselves if they enhance an institution, or bring it into disrepute, by allowing something that corrupts and mocks it to flourish unchecked. You may end up with a product that is not worth protecting, and increase the numbers of people who can only feel bitterness and cynicism towards it. It is unlikely that the generations of past and present incest survivors have been persuaded that the family is the touchstone of their nation's highest moral values. Those who wish to convince people of that must ask themselves if they are going about it in the best way.

Some readers may feel my arguments are too political, theoretical and biased.

Most of us are brought up with the naive belief that research is neutral and scientific. This is rarely true, especially with social and psychological research: there are twenty ways of interpreting the same evidence. Current professional thinking and writing on incest is neither neutral, untheoretical nor apolitical, it merely pretends to be. It makes numerous assumptions about human nature, male and female sexuality, class, the family and the social order, which have had profound consequences for policy, and for the lives of vulnerable people. 'Children are very sexy and invite it' is a theory. 'They don't mind it in the lower class subculture' is a theory. We are not changing a neutral subject into a biased, political one, for it is already that. We are asking if it makes more sense to place a different theoretical interpretation on the evidence in front of us.

Unless social workers and other professionals have some kind of theory about the problem they are dealing with, they cannot take any useful positive action. At present most are either basing their judgments on existing theories such as 'Legal proceedings are known to damage the child, so I won't report'. Or they are doing nothing because they have no theory at all: 'This is all so complex and interwoven a family situation that we would need to know much more before we could understand'. This refusal to take and follow a positive line has simply caused paralysis and a sense of inadequacy. Taking a broad view and avoiding judgment has got us precisely nowhere.

It is time for social workers and other caring agencies to stop justifying incest, or dithering about this extremely complex and delicate family dynamic. Their first, unequivocal aim should be to protect the child, and find a way of stopping the incest permanently.

Facts and Figures

Historically, most societies throughout the world have practised some form of prohibition against incest, or sexual relations between people considered 'near of kin'.

Webster's *Third International Dictionary* defines incest as: 'Sexual intercourse or inbreeding between closely related individuals especially when they are related or regarded as related ... within degrees wherein marriage is prohibited by law or custom'.

But in fact forbidden degrees vary widely, and do not always follow rules for marriage. In recent years there has also been growing pressure for reform of incest law in Scotland and England, on the grounds that it is anachronistic, inappropriate or inadequate. This has already led to Scottish changes which move the emphasis towards the abuse of trust by adults against children. There has also been wider debate, in this country and internationally, on the whole meaning and definition of incest and child sexual abuse.

The arguments have political implications for the approach to sexual abuse and its treatment, and have sometimes proved divisive among professionals and campaigners.

Till 1986 Scottish incest law derived from the Incest Act of 1567, which was based on Biblical authority: 'Whatsoever person or persons they be that abuse their body with such persons in degree as God's word has expressly forbidden ... shall be punished.' Scots law covered relationships both by blood (consanguinity) and by marriage (affinity). But adoptive ties were not included, and the position of illegitimate children was unclear.

Incest cases could only be tried in the High Court. The maximum sentence was life imprisonment, but this was seldom imposed. The Scottish Law Commission's 1971–76 statistics showed that average prison sentences for adult offenders were two to four years.

Incest did, and still does, involve penetration of the female's body, which may be hard to prove and means children who have suffered prolonged assaults not involving intercourse cannot find protection in incest law.

Other laws may be invoked for instance lewd, indecent and libidinous practices. This charge tends to be brought where the victim has not yet reached the age of 12. Section five of the Sexual Offences (Scotland) Act 1976 provides that anyone using such behaviour towards a girl aged between 12 and 16 shall be liable to a jail sentence of not more than two years.

Current English law dates from the Punishment of Incest Act 1908, consolidated in the Sexual Offences Act 1956. Like Scots law it must involve penetration, but it covers only blood relationships, and children need not be legitimate. However, for no clear reason it excludes incest between uncle and niece, or aunt and nephew.

The offence is triable on indictment only and prosecutions must have the authority of the Director of Public Prosecutions. There is a maximum of seven years imprisonment, or life if the girl involved is under 13.

On Hall-Williams' statistics, one half to three quarters of convicted offenders are jailed, with average sentences three to four years. On figures quoted by the Criminal Law Revision Committee, in 1977 one father was jailed for more than seven years, 11 for five to seven years, and 82 for 18 months to five years. In English law children under 16 may also find protection under offences of unlawful sexual intercourse, and gross indecency with children.

Concern about the current state of incest law encouraged the Secretary of State for Scotland to ask the Scottish Law Commission in 1981 to review it, and make suggestions for reform. In England the Criminal Law Revision Committee (CLRC) presented its fifteenth report, on sexual offences, in 1984.

Pressure for reform had several causes. Some people felt prohibitions based on religious strictures were anachronistic and no longer relevant to modern society. Sometimes they produced incongruous results. For instance in Scotland, marriage and incest prohibitions have been slightly out of step since the Marriage (Scotland) Act 1977 shortened the list of forbidden degrees.

The 'libertarian' lobby was especially concerned about rules that could erode the civil rights of consenting sexual partners in modern society. The National Council for Civil Liberties (NCCL) in its evidence to the Criminal Law Revision Committee, said the crime of incest should be abolished. 'In our view no benefit accrues to anyone by making incest a crime when committed by mutually consenting persons over the age of consent'. They also urged that the over 14s should be capable of giving consent to sexual intercourse. In cases of parent–child incest the law of assault should operate, though the NCCL then warned against the 'damage' court proceedings could do to a child.

Other critics have taken a very different view. Publicised cases of adult relatives who wish to marry are rare, they argue, and incest law is ineffective because it does not confront the bulk of the problem, which is, in Fran Wasoff's words, 'sexual exploitation of a child by a person responsible for her care and nurturance.' As such, genetic arguments are a side issue, since what is at stake is not the blood relationship but the abuse of a social relationship.

Likewise Professor J. K. Mason wanted basic revulsion to incest defined in a way acceptable in modern terms, i.e. 'the ultimate offence is exploitation of a captive population which because of its submissive position, is not only virtually unable to refuse, but is also unable to express an autonomous consent.'

Stress on the need to protect vulnerable young people means age limits, strict blood ties or the exact nature of the sexual acts become less important. Thus with Professor Mason, the Scottish Council for Civil Liberties urged that the existing incest law be replaced with an offence called 'sexual abuse of care'. This would cover unwelcome sexual acts other than penetration, and would protect all young people, including foster children, in a position of trust and care within the family.

Criticisms of this kind clearly influenced the Scottish and English reviews. In December 1981 the Scottish Law Commission published its final report. The main recommendations were that incest be retained as a separate offence; prohibitions should be based on blood ties and include illegitimate children; the only exceptions to the consanguinity rule would be adopted children. It should be a separate offence for any step-parent to have intercourse with a stepchild under 16.

The Incest and Related Offences (Scotland) Act, enacted in 1986, closely follows these recommendations. Forbidden degrees include parents and children, grandparents and grandchildren, and great grandparents and great grandchildren. Aunts, uncles, nephews and nieces are also included. Forbidden relationships by adoption cover parents and their adopted, or formerly adopted, children.

A step-parent is guilty of an offence with a stepchild who is under 21 or who has lived in the same household before reaching the age of 18. Proceedings may take place in the High Court (maximum sentence life imprisonment) or in the sheriff court (maximum two years).

English proposals by the CLRC include adoptive ties, but still mysteriously exclude uncles and aunts. Brother–sister intercourse should cease to be an offence of incest where both have reached the age of 21. There should be a separate offence of unlawful sexual intercourse with a stepchild under 21. Sentencing policy would remain as before, including the need for consent by the Director of Public Prosecutions.

The Scottish Law Commission still placed a lot of emphasis on genetic arguments against incest like possible handicap in the offspring. The Criminal Law Revision Committee made the following interesting comment in its report, which increasingly reflects professional thinking on the importance of genetic factors:

> The precise degree of genetic risk is not very important to a consideration of the justification for an offence of incest. Society does not yet prohibit sexual intercourse in other circumstances where there is a high genetic risk of abnormality ... and we are very anxious about the implications of any proposal that it should. The fact is that in relation to incest there are other very strong grounds for prohibition which still apply even where pregnancy would be avoided. That in our view is where the emphasis should properly be placed rather than concentrate on the strict blood-ties issues.

The new stress on the need to protect vulnerable children will be welcomed by many people throughout Britain. But serious doubts must remain about whether the reforms will reduce other major problems like gross under-reporting, low prosecution rates, and low conviction rates.

Better reporting depends partly on good, clear legal procedures, but more on the creation of a safe social climate, and those problems will be touched on in many other places in this book. Low prosecution rates also depend considerably on the social and political attitudes of professionals, and these too will be discussed in detail elsewhere. But prosecutions and convictions are also affected by legal rules and procedures which have been virtually untouched by the reform plans. Many campaigners believe they must be addressed before the courts in this country can become really effective in protecting those who suffer sexual abuse.

Peter Ferguson, Depute Reporter to the children's panels in Highland Region, has listed some Scottish examples to support his view that 'the criminal legal system and procedures are singularly ill-equipped to provide appropriate child protection or a framework for treatment'. Only 30 per cent of incest cases reported to Scottish police between 1951 and 1978 resulted in convictions. Hall-Williams' figures showed less than half of reported English cases were prosecuted to conviction each year.

First the courts demand a high standard of proof, which includes an admission by the accused or forensic or circumstantial evidence. Yet the acts are by their nature done in secret, and medical examinations will only give forensic evidence if intercourse took place very recently. It appears that a parent accused of sexual offences against their child can even refuse permission for the medical examination to take place.

In Scotland a wife cannot be forced to give evidence against her husband though her evidence may be crucial in these cases: 'It is not uncommon for wives to decline to give evidence, and this usually heralds the collapse of the case.'

It can take three months to a year for the case to reach court. This simply invites retraction of the allegations: 'Pressures from abuser, hostile family, or uncaring and dismissive agencies who appear sceptical or blaming will combine, with the realisation of the enormity of the changes the allegation has brought, unless consistent support is available to the victim.'

The formal court setting and the treatment meted out by defence lawyers militates against the child being believed even when she does reach court. The defence won't be based on mistaken identity or alibi, but on the child's allegation as malicious or fantastic. So her character and behaviour may be torn to shreds, and if she has been misbehaving as a result of the abuse this will appear as further proof that she is unreliable.

Incest cases are excluded from the limited protection raped and sexually abused women are now supposed to get from cross-examination about their character and sex lives, since evidence law was changed in the Miscellaneous Provisions Scotland Act (January 1986). Indeed the incest victim is in 'double jeopardy', says Ferguson. Both parties to intercourse are said to commit incest and the victim, if over eight years, is an 'accomplice' whose evidence must be viewed with special scrutiny.

These problems all point to the fact that changing incest law is not in itself enough to ensure fair legal treatment for young people at risk. They also suggest that there is an important role for concerned people in the legal profession to lead the way in suggesting imaginative and workable reforms which will still protect the basic rights of all parties in incest cases.

On the whole issue of definitions, professionals may now be

more willing to broaden their view of what constitutes incestuous abuse. But restricted and legalistic definitions have caused suspicion and antagonism among many campaigners, especially feminists and members of incest survivor groups themselves.

They feel these definitions have been used as excuses for playing down, or taking no action against, forms of abuse that do not involve penetration. Survivor groups have listed dozens of abuses faced by their members, including pornographic photo sessions and coercion on brothers or sisters to watch the abuse of a child. They also feel the stress on blood ties reinforces the tendency to see incest as a 'family dynamic' where all family members are in some way responsible for what has happened.

The London-based Incest Survivors Campaign has put forward the following definition of incest, which has been broadly adopted by other groups:

> The sexual molestation of a child by any older person perceived as a figure of trust or authority – parents, relatives (whether natural or adoptive), family friends, youth leaders and teachers, etc. The questions of blood-relationship and taboo are red herrings which obscure the central issue: the exploitation of children's trust and obedience by irresponsible adults. Incest is the abuse of power. (ISC 1981)

Confusion and disagreement over definitions have tended to increase because in recent years there has been far more widespread debate on child sexual abuse in general which includes assaults by strangers. It has finally been recognised as a major social problem.

Survivor groups have the right to define incest as they choose. In this particular book I shall work broadly on a more restricted definition along the lines proposed by the psychotherapist Susan Forward:

> Any overtly sexual contact between people who are either closely related or perceive themselves to be ... if that special trust that exists between a child and parent figure or sibling is violated by a sexual act, that act becomes incestuous.

It is important to make clear the reasons for restricting the definition here. Firstly, assaults on children and young people (mainly female) by babysitters, family acquaintances, teachers or youth leaders are widespread and have barely yet been taken seriously. They may often have some similar damaging effects to abuse by family members. But the danger about including them in the category of incest is that it becomes very easy for critics who doubt the prevalence of family sexual abuse to discount any statistics which campaigners produce. They can allege that new figures are unreliable because all manner of relationships have been included. But in the battle to force society to take action, statistics are a basic and a vital weapon.

I believe it is more useful and effective to gather separate information on abuse by other people in positions of trust. Often this will emerge in the course of research into abuse in the family. For instance the Irish Council for Civil Liberties has in its own study (see page 105) found widespread evidence of assaults by baby-sitters, especially teenage boys. Secondly, emphasis on family assaults does not necessarily play into the hands of uncritical apologists for the family unit. On the contrary it may encourage people to ask what is wrong with existing beliefs about how husbands, wives and children should behave, if these beliefs permit so much sexual abuse. Nothing should be allowed to obscure the fact that the majority of survivors suffered at the hands of a father figure or brother. It is true that survivor groups must be open to anyone who feels she has suffered similar feelings and reactions to other members of the group, and who finds helpful ways used by the group to restore self respect and assert control. Members make the choice: groups will be appropriate for some and not for others. In any case it is often very difficult to make clear distinctions between an uncle and a close family friend: assumptions of trust may be similar.

None the less it still seems very important to stress to professional workers that abuse of trust within the family seems to have particularly damaging effects that can last throughout a person's life and affect all other relationships. This book is only one source of such evidence. It is important not just because it is true, but because traditionally professionals have ignored or played down such abuse just because it takes place within the family. Messages have to be clear, and they have to be unequivocal. There is no good place for sexual abuse. But the family is the most destructive place of all.

Which family members usually commit incest?

The great majority of incest cases made known to the police and other agencies involve daughter and father (or father figure, including stepfather). The preponderance of father–daughter incest has been noted in countries throughout the world: for instance in his classic study, *Sex and Repression in Savage Society*, Malinowski wrote that among the Trobrianders, 'Father-daughter incest seems to be incomparably more frequent than that between mother and son'.

Yet despite all the statistics, attempts to explain why father-daughter incest prevails in such a striking way have been until recently scarce in research literature. (The feminist analysis of the patriarchal family is one example of a direct attempt to confront the question.) Nor, despite intense efforts, have researchers ever managed to find more than a handful of mother-son cases.

Of the 200 court cases examined by Weinberg in Chicago, more than 75 per cent involved father and daughter, one per cent mother and son. In Kubo's 36 cases, the figures were 31 and 2. Forty of the 52 court cases studied by the Scottish Law Commission were father-daughter, while 72 per cent of the convictions involved this relationship in the Home Office study of English incest offences in 1973.

Forward suggests that in the USA 75 per cent of reported incest cases involve fathers and daughters. This type of incest predominated in the 112 families studied by Blair and Rita Justice, where there were only two mother-son cases.

As numerous incest survivors in many countries have spoken openly of their experiences in recent years, it has become clear that much of this abuse has involved stepfathers, foster fathers, a mother's live-in boyfriend, and so on. It is interesting to note that David Finkelhor, who has researched extensively on child sexual abuse, believes that while most of the increased reporting of incest does not reflect a real growth in incidence, abuse by father-substitutes may be on the increase. This is because they have more access to children due to changes in social habits because with more divorces, more women set up home with another partner.

The eldest girl in the family is often the most vulnerable to abuse by a father, especially where she has been put in the mother's role in other ways (e.g. expected to cook, clean and provide household services).

But fathers may abuse several daughters in turn. In 30 per cent of Hall-Williams' cases there were two children involved. A Harborview study (USA) found that 34 per cent of siblings of the primary client were also abused. Lukianowicz describes a Northern Ireland man who abused two of his daughters and his five granddaughters. One of these was also his daughter. Accounts from many incest survivors describe their intense fears for their younger sisters and their attempts to protect these children from abuse.

It is often within these 'multiple incest' situations that father–son incest is found. This took place in five per cent of cases studied by Maisch. The Kempes quote an example of suspected multiple incest where the same gonorrhea strain was found in an adult man, his three stepdaughters and his nine-year-old stepson.

It is now widely accepted that most sexual abuse of males is committed by heterosexual males. Existing studies would suggest that boys are more vulnerable to abuse from those outside the family than from relatives. It is often claimed that males are even more reluctant than females to admit in later life that they were sexually abused. A MORI poll for Channel 4 in 1984 suggested one in eight girls and one in 12 boys had suffered some form of abuse in childhood: in making any comparisons between males and females, however, it is important that statisticians make quite clear what forms and levels of abuse are being talked about, and do not fudge differences in experience.

Most remaining cases involve adult men and female children. This pattern is similar to sexual offences in general against children. The de Francis study suggested more than 90 per cent of victims were female and more than 95 per cent of offenders were male. The Harborview project has found similar figures.

In Maisch's German incest study, fathers or stepfathers and daughters, or grandfathers and grand-daughters, accounted for 90 per cent of the total. Forward says about 10 per cent of her cases have involved grandfathers: similar percentages were found in a Tsai and Wagner study of 118 sexually molested women (1979). Again, numerous published accounts by survivors dent the image of the benign and helpless grandfather: a particularly savage case, which produced one woman's psychosis, is described in Forward.

Many researchers and professional workers have believed brother–sister incest is very common, if not the major form, though this has not been based on hard statistics. It has also been assumed that this is less damaging, if not positively benign, because it has been widely seen as the kind of child and adolescent experiment which very many people indulge in, to their later embarrassment or amusement.

But an increasing number of accounts from incest survivors suggest that most brother–sister incest involves an older boy who coerces a younger girl. (Forward says older brother and younger sister is the commonest form of sibling incest.) The Incest Survivors Campaign in London say their own questionnaires uncovered a surprisingly high level of such abuse. It often seems to be accompanied by physical violence. This seems an area where comfortable folklore needs to be challenged by more hard research, which may lead professional agencies to take a different view of 'adolescent experiment' and its effects.

Incest between uncle and niece also seems to involve considerable disparities in age. We can thus see how small a role 'mutually consenting adults' play generally in incestuous behaviour.

How old are those involved in incest?

It is often claimed that men are tempted to commit incest when their daughters become sexually appealing in puberty. For instance, in his review of the incest literature, Henderson writes: 'When a father is confronted with an increasingly frustrating marriage and an increasingly attractive adolescent daughter, overt incest may occur.'

But this theory is simply not borne out, either by court cases or by reports from clinicians and survivors. Incestuous abuse usually starts well before the girl reaches puberty. Health visitors have told me they have seen abused children under two years: the Irish Council for Civil Liberties study has uncovered cases where men abused babies of a few months old. The Harborview project has found about one in five of sexually abused children to be six years old or younger.

According to the Kempes, who spent 20 years working with abused children, 'Incestuous relationships may begin at the toddler age and continue into adult life. The median age . . . has been between nine and ten years.'

For the women in Herman and Hirschman's study six to nine was a common age range of first abuse, while Lukianowicz found this to be eight and a half years. In more than half of the Scottish Law Commission's father–daughter cases, girls were 12 or younger. All this means, of course, that in the great majority of incest cases physical damage and injury is likely to have happened. The extensive age range suggests that it is mistaken to look for some characteristic in the girls, which could somehow precipitate abuse. Instead we must ask what it is about the offender which makes him prepared to initiate sex with babies, young children or teenagers.

There have also been attempts to find a typical age range for offenders. This must rely heavily on cases brought before courts and treatment programmes. The Scottish Law Commission's figures suggest most offenders are between 29 and 40. Hall-Williams' subjects ranged from 30 to 50 years, Lukianowicz' from 29 to 41. Such figures tend to strengthen the image of men whose marriages have grown stale or who are in some kind of mid-life crisis: but we must ask seriously how useful such statistics are.

Incest offenders are among the most reluctant of all groups to come forward publicly. They do not write their life histories in popular magazines, and we have to rely for statistics on the tiny proportion who are 'caught'. It is more useful to note the wide disparities in age reported by survivors, and the growing evidence that teenage boys as a group are vulnerable to becoming sexual abusers. The more important question to be asked is why men of all ages abuse members of their families.

How long does the incest last?

Rape and other sexual attacks by strangers, however traumatic, are usually single events. But family sexual abuse may continue for years, with intercourse taking place daily, or several times a week.

Most researchers have found that father–daughter incest is likely to be prolonged. Maisch noted that 71 per cent of his 1500 cases had lasted more than a year; Lukianowicz found a mean of eight years in her sample. Harborview found 29 per cent of their cases continuing for one to five years and nine per cent for more than five years.

Noreen Winchester, the Belfast girl who stabbed her father to death at the age of 19, had suffered her father's beatings and sexual assaults, often several times a day, since she was 11.

Hundreds of accounts of survivors' experiences have been published in recent years, and the majority suggest that abuse continued for several years. By their nature father figure–daughter abuses are likely to be more prolonged than other forms of incest, because of the father's special authority and the child's dependence on him. But the assumption that other relationships will be transient is too glib: Lukianowicz found the average duration of uncle–niece abuse was as much as two years. Brother–sister relationships ranged from two to fourteen years, with an average of four years.

It should not be assumed that there is some direct correlation between the duration of sexual abuse and the damage caused by it. Many women have reported a serious effect on their lives from short episodes of abuse: constant fear of recurrence, even if this does not happen, can cripple a childhood. None the less we can see how many survivors have had to sacrifice a part of childhood, which many people consider precious and which cannot be re-lived, to exploitation, pain, fear and secrecy.

The second caveat is that there is not a typical or average dur-ation for incest, which has something to do with the relationship per se. Duration has been strongly connected with the numerous social problems involved in exposing it and gaining help. Incestuous abuse lasts as long as it does because nobody steps in to prevent it. Many abusers will continue what they are doing in-definitely – for as long, that is, as they are allowed to.

What social backgrounds do those who practise incest come from?

The idea that incest only happens in the lower classes and among people with social problems is widespread among researchers, professionals and the general public.

The importance of poverty, poor housing, overcrowding and social marginality has been claimed by many writers, including Flugel, Guttmacher, Reimer and Rhinehart. Szabo found that most of his 96 cases came from a working class or lower working class background, with a heavy incidence of alcoholism. Like some other writers, he also stressed the importance of isolation: most of his sample lived in remote mountainous areas.

Lukianowicz pointed out that the typical research profile of the incestuous father suggested he came from a broken home, had little schooling and worked sporadically at labouring jobs. The number of lower working class families in her own sample (19 out of 26) encouraged her to put forward the influential theory that incest is an accepted practice in the lower class 'subculture'. Studies on the background of convicted incest offenders also tend to support the idea that it is a working class or 'problem family' crime where the participants often suffer from alcoholism, mental illness or general 'inadequacy'.

But other researchers have challenged these findings. Cavallin thought there was 'little evidence that deprivation, low intelli-gence, overcrowding and isolation are significant contributory factors' in incest.

The Scottish Law Commission summarises the major flaw of popular views:

Their (the underprivileged) predominance among the statistics is probably more a reflection of the sampling procedures used in the studies than a true picture of what actually occurs. The studies are generally drawn from criminal and court records and it is accepted that the majority of people appearing in criminal courts are of lower social position, borderline economic means and live in crowded living quarters.

Likewise Henderson talks about 'unfortunate' sampling procedures which have led socio-economic variables to be 'heavily biased'. Lukianowicz, for example, drew her samples from the very places where disadvantaged people would predominate, like an approved school and a state mental hospital.

Social work agencies, who largely service the poor and people with special problems, are also likely to land with biased samples. Problems like alcoholism, mental illness or violent behaviour also bring families quickly to official attention, often causing the incest secret to be blown accidentally.

In contrast to the lower class findings, Cavallin, Wiener, and Browning and Boatman drew their cases from the middle class to lower middle class groups. The Justices found that many incestuous fathers were respected citizens who included judges, doctors, teachers and foremen. The Kempes wrote:

> Most of the youngsters we now see ... represent the children of professionals and white and blue collar workers, as well as the poor, in a way that reflects a true cross-section of the community.

Maisch found that 77 per cent of the families he studied were 'comfortable' financially.

Writers and researchers are increasingly commenting that incestuous fathers tend to be more strongly religious than normal, even though this sits ill with the promiscuous drunken layabout theory. Religious fathers' abuse is often linked with their unwillingness to commit adultery by going outside the family, and in one Irish case reported to me, a father genuinely believed this would be a greater sin than abusing his daughter.

Catholics have been seen as particularly vulnerable to abuse and abusing. In a remarkably offensive paragraph Renvoize (1982) quotes *The Times*' opinion that Catholics are vastly overrepresented among criminals, alcoholics, drug addicts and nightclub strippers. Since alcoholism and drug addiction are linked to sexual abuse we may fairly expect incest to be over-represented among English and Welsh Catholics, she says.

Leaving aside the confusion here (Catholic crime, etc. is closely linked to their socio-economic position as a group in Britain) the following comments seem appropriate. Incest survivors will welcome the new awareness that highly respectable and religious people may also be abusers. They have known this for centuries. It is time the taboo was lifted from open discussion about how sexual repression, perverted guilt, and notions about different degrees of sexual sin may actually encourage incestuous abuse.

But it is also dangerous to make glib assumptions about cause and effect. For instance, the crucial factor may not be the beliefs of a particular religion, but rather the strongly patriarchal and authoritarian thread which runs through several denominations and sects, and justifies extreme dominance by a father over his family. Any set of religious or political beliefs which does this may increase the likelihood of sexual abuse. It should also be said, of course, that strong religious convictions may equally well prevent fathers from initiating sexual abuse.

Thus Forward, who treated 300 incest cases in her practice, concluded:

> (the families) come from every economic, cultural, racial, educational, religious and geographical background. They are doctors, policemen, prostitutes, secretaries, artists and merchants. They are heterosexual, bisexual and homosexual. They are happily married and four-times divorced ... they are emotionally stable and they have multiple personalities.

The message is clear – that incest can happen in all types of family. Respectable ones are merely better at concealing it, and are less likely to come to the attention of social agencies. In many of the cases quoted above, incest had remained a secret for many years, usually well into the victim's adulthood.

Comparing this picture with general sexual abuse statistics, we can recall that 24 per cent of Kinsey's white, middle class female sample reported childhood experiences with an adult male, and 6 per cent specifically with a relative.

What are some of the consequences for child victims of incest?

Pregnancy
Pregnancy resulting from incest is always likely to be underreported and under-estimated. But even the figures we have suggest a rate between 10 and 20 per cent of cases.

For instance nine per cent of offences in Hall-Williams' sample came to light because of pregnancy. This was discovered in 16 of the cases studied by the SLC, and in about 20 per cent of Maisch's German sample. Comparing this situation with general child abuse statistics, we find that pregnancy resulted from the offence in 29 of the 263 cases studied by de Francis – more than 10 per cent.

Reasons for under-estimation include miscarriages, abortions and falsely attributed paternity: where responsibility is left unknown or placed upon someone else (like a boyfriend, or the casual contact of a 'promiscuous' teenage girl).

Cases are also suppressed by the media. Recently a woman reporter in the north of England, who had gone to report cases in a busy courthouse, found herself at an incest trial where a girl of 12 had given birth to her father's child. She had concealed the pregnancy until a few days before the birth: her emotional ordeal can only be guessed at.

The judge spoke of this 'incredible and shocking case' but the reporter's news editor said he could not possibly print the story. The local radio station also rejected it, saying it was not their policy to publicise such things.

In a recent Scottish case which was reported in the Press, an Islay father was jailed after his pre-teenage daughter gave birth to a severely handicapped child who died a few hours later. A year before, she had endured the same experience, though it did not appear to prompt anyone to step in and protect her.

As the age of puberty diminishes, many girls nowadays can conceive at 11, before some even understand about sex and conception, and long before they have the emotional maturity to cope with such a momentous event, or with the care of a child.

Many offspring of incestuous unions are physically and mentally normal. But the chances of abnormality is appreciably higher than in non-incestuous relationships. (Genetic arguments, of course, have been important in the debate for and against the legalising of incest, and there is a substantial literature on the subject.) Studies of incestuous unions, or marriages between close relatives, have found a higher risk of early death, infant death, and major physical or mental defects. Seemanova's well-known Czech study showed 'an unmistakeable effect of inbreeding on infant mortality, congenital malformations and intelligence level.'

This means that in addition to coping with the pregnancy, incest victims or their relatives may also have to spend years looking after a handicapped child, who may itself suffer because of the disability. The economic hardships faced by single-parent fam-

ilies, and the stigma and disadvantage which still burden illegitimate children, are likely to pile up still more problems in the
future for mother and offspring alike.

Physical damage and injury

Not the least remarkable aspect of an extensive incest literature is
the near-absence of comment on physical damage to victims
despite the extreme youth of so many girls involved. Most researchers and professionals do not even seem to have considered
it, let alone searched for it or discussed it. This may reflect a lack
of imagination among writers who are overwhelmingly male, but
women researchers have often shared their silence.

Apart from the apparent feeling that physical damage is not
worth attention, there are other reasons why it figures so little in
the literature.

First, most survivors only come to professional attention long
after pre-pubertal injuries have happened and healed. Thus VD is
the only physical problem regularly mentioned in research, because it is likely to recur and show itself in older girls. Secondly,
a parent is unlikely to report pre-pubertal injuries to a doctor, for
fear of awkward questions at the surgery. Thirdly, even when reported, these injuries may not be recognised as the result of
sexual abuse.

In their research on wife beating, Dobash and Dobash found
that only three per cent of all injuries received by their inter-
viewees had been reported to a doctor. Even then GPs only discussed the beatings in a quarter of cases, and rarely made
referrals to other agencies. Many doctors felt wife battering was
not their concern. Hints of incest are still less likely to be taken up
or recognised by doctors, who may also shy away from the problem through embarrassment or abhorrence.

Social workers may also fail to take up the clues, as one authority on child abuse told Weber:

Many social workers will report and talk about bruises but
are unwilling to press further to determine if this is a case of
sexual abuse, in which the bruise is only a secondary characteristic.

Silence and lack of referral means we have to guess at physical
damage wrought by incest by looking at studies of general child
sex abuse.

For instance the Kempes highlight a case where a six year old girl was raped by her babysitter. She suffered a one-inch vaginal tear, caught VD and had to be hospitalised for emotional as well as medical reasons.

In recent years a (largely American) medical literature on child sexual abuse has grown up. This lists forms of damage commonly found among child victims: syphilis, genital herpes, non-specific vulvo-vaginitis, vaginal tears, ulceronduloar lesions, and other genital injuries and infections. Much of this literature is critical of non-recognition and non-collaboration, urges professional alertness to signs and symptoms, and lays down guidelines for action by supportive services.

The abuse may manifest itself in subtler physical ways, as Forward notes:

> The victim may often manifest her guilt in psychosomatic symptoms – most often migraines. Many of the symptoms often associated with tension may appear, including stomach ailments, skin disorders, and disabling aches and pains. Though not every victim I have seen has suffered all of these symptoms, I have yet to see a victim who does not suffer from a combination of several of them.

Violence which accompanies the incestuous act can also cause injury and damage.

Many incestuous fathers win their daughters' compliance without overt violence. They may use a variety of threats and rewards, or simply exploit their position of authority.

A Harborview study of 593 children who were sexually molested between 1977 and 1979 found more than half the sample were victims of family abuse. Of these, they found 16 per cent had been coerced by physical force, 16 per cent were threatened with force, and 63 per cent were coerced by adult authority. In one programme for victims of sexual abuse set up in Minnesota, it was estimated that additional physical abuse to the incest occurred in nearly half the families. In 39 per cent of the families the wife was also physically abused.

The role played by overt violence, which will reappear in discussion later on authoritarian fathers, has been commented on by a number of writers. For instance the Kempes state:

> In pre-adolescence and early adolescence the association between physical abuse and sexual exploitation is sometimes striking, if rarely discussed, and it is not uncommon for adolescent girls we observe ... to suffer from both.

In Hall-Williams' study, violence and threats were known to accompany the offence in 12 per cent of cases.

The extremes to which this violence can go have been described by Tormes:

> There follow several examples of father behaviour described by 13 mothers and in every instance corroborated by the child victim: . . . burning the child with hot irons, chasing the mother out of the house with a gun; . . . locking mother or children in closets while he sexually abused the child victim . . . forcing sexual intercourse with the child in the mother's presence . . . etc.

During Noreen Winchester's eight years of sexual abuse, she was beaten regularly by her father, as was her mother, and several other children.

Information from co-ordinators of battered women's refuges in Britain and Ireland also suggest that beatings and sexual abuse often go together. They said that after women had found the confidence to talk about their lives, they would regularly admit that their husbands had either committed incest with their daughters, or had tried to. (This was often the last straw which made mothers leave with their children.) One co-ordinator said she had 'hardly met a battered woman' in her refuge who had not admitted this eventually.

The constant presence, or threat, of overt violence in the family provides, of course, another good reason why mother and victim might be what Lukianowicz calls overtolerant of the incest for many years.

Recalling general child sex abuse statistics, we find that in de Francis' sample, 60 per cent of child victims were coerced by direct force or threat of bodily harm, while in 25 per cent of cases the lure was based on the child's loyalty and affection for a friend or relative.

Psychological damage

In contrast to their near-silence about physical effects, the vast majority of researchers and professionals discuss the presence or possibility of psychological damage in incest victims. This is not to say that they all see incest as the cause of damage as we shall discover later.

Some of the problems listed here have been found in the girls referred because of incest. In other cases, and more often, the process has worked in reverse. Women presenting severe psychological or behavioural difficulties have later admitted a history of incest. Thus psychiatrists, social workers, marriage guidance counsellors and court workers will remark time and again how often they discovered such a history in their clients. In the last few years, checklists or guidelines for the detection of child sexual abuse have been developed by survivor groups, sexual assault projects, prevention schemes and social agencies.

This discussion is a summary, and many of the issues, such as why girls might react in a certain way, and how 'experts' have interpreted their behaviour, will be examined in more detail later.

Some influential writers have denied that incest causes psychological harm to pre-pubertal children. But this view has been challenged, especially by practising clinicians and therapists.

For instance Lewis and Sarrel found anxiety symptoms ranging from enuresis, speech problems and nightmares to 'phobic and obsessional states'. The Kempes found child sex abuse victims suffered fear states and night terrors; clinging behaviour and developmental regression; insomnia, hysteria and sudden school failure. Some also ran away from home.

Given that children referred to child psychiatrists very often show just these symptoms, we may wonder how many undiagnosed young victims of incest there still are.

There is wider agreement that incest is psychologically damaging to adolescents, and most of the literature concentrates on teenagers. Certain problems appear with great frequency and consistency.

Depression, neuroses and suicidal tendencies are the main causes of referral for 'unrevealed' incest survivors, and they often continue throughout adult life.

There is also apparent sexual promiscuity and a higher than normal tendency to take up prostitution. In their study 'Incest as a Causative Factor in Antisocial Behaviour', Benward and Densen-Gerber found a strong association between incest and both promiscuity and prostitution.

Flugel quoted an official report in which 51 of 103 prostitutes examined claimed that their first sexual experience was with their fathers. Forward noted an American study by James, where 25 per cent of an interview sample of prostitutes had been incest victims. Other disorders which are likely to bring teenage girls and older women to the attention of psychologists and psychiatrists.

There is growing evidence that eating disorders like anorexia nervosa or bulmonia may be signs of reaction to incestuous abuse. Many people who suffer these will not be incest survivors, but the possibility should be checked. It is being written about increasingly both by survivors and by mental health workers, and has strong links with feelings of self-disgust and lack of control over one's own body. After one talk on incest which I gave, a woman approached me and said five out of seven members of her compulsive eating self-help group were incest survivors.

Agrophobia, which is mainly suffered by women, should also alert people to the possibility of reaction to incestuous abuse. This has been linked to the personal fear or even terror which many women suffered, often for years, while the abuse continued. Other signs are behaviour disturbances including truancy, running away from home, delinquency, drug and alcohol abuse.

The Kempes note 'one half of our runaway girls (seen at the treatment centre) were involved in sexual abuse.' Odyssey House, an American residential programme with centres throughout the USA, reports that 44 per cent of its female drug addicts were sexually abused in childhood. John Silverson, a Minneapolis therapist who treated over 500 teenage drug addicts, has put the figure at 70 per cent.

Many women show a whole range of the problems discussed above. Lukianowicz describes a girl who practised chaotic promiscuity alternating with bouts of depression and suicide attempts. Mary, described by Stucker, ran away from home, became a drug addict, got pregnant, became a prostitute to pay for her drug habit, and attempted suicide. Some girls develop manifest psychosis, including schizophrenia.

Others show a revulsion against sex, which persists throughout adult life contributing to marital problems. Experts call this frigidity.

Incest survivors persistently describe how they tried to cut themselves off mentally from the act, freeze up or pretend it wasn't happening. This can spread into other areas of life besides sex, causing feelings of social isolation, inability to communicate or get close to other people. Estrangement from the mother can occur, or even open hostility and bitterness. 'This is a near-universal finding among incest victims, who feel deeply betrayed by their mothers.'

Self-disgust is compounded by intense shame and guilt. Most girls appear to feel degraded and worthless. 'Think of the lowest thing in the world, and whatever it is, I'm lower' one victim, a competent psychiatric nurse, told Forward. 'I felt bad and dirty all the time,' said Noreen Winchester.

Victims in Herman and Hirschman's study called themselves whores and witches: several felt they deserved to be beaten and abused. Most women feel they must be to blame for what happened. Exposure only compounds guilt when the girl feels responsible for

> public retribution with the firm expectation of total family disruption, unemployment and economic disaster, loss of family and friends for the victim and probably incarceration for the perpetrator.

The legal process can be particularly painful and humiliating, with merciless cross-examination before a courtroom of strangers. Even if the abuse hasn't made an impact, says Dorothy Ross, 'by the time the system gets through with her it has become the most important thing that ever happened in her life.'

So there is no escape from the double-bind: the psychological burden of keeping the incest secret may be intolerable, the traumas involved in revealing it equally so.

How common is incest?

Knowledge about the nature of incest, and the damage it causes, does not by itself guarantee public concern and action. People may console themselves with the belief that any suffering affects a tiny minority of the population. The sense of urgency they bring to tackling the problem will depend crucially on what they believe about the frequency of incestuous abuse.

If we rely on criminal statistics, as many professionals and researchers have done, we will indeed see incest as a minuscule social problem. For instance the Scottish Law Commission showed that between 1951 and 1978, incest reporting stayed remarkably stable, varying from 18 to 49 per year in a population of 6 million. In contrast reported rapes increased from 18 in 1951 to 166 in 1978; assaults with intent to ravish from 18 to 164; and indecent assaults from 287 to 946.

In England and Wales, according to the Scottish Law Commission, 'the number of (incest) offences made known has each year been between 237 and 337, with a movement in more recent years back to the former total'. These low official figures seem to be echoed in most countries. If estimates are based on convictions, figures are lower still because police discretion, official doubts about intervention, and problems about corroborative evidence produce a low prosecution rate.

If we reject these figures as inadequate, we must also accept that we cannot offer readers, or clamouring researchers, precise alternatives. Till all the many taboos on reporting are broken no one can gauge the exact frequency, nor 'prove' that four per cent, or nine per cent, of British women have a history of incestuous abuse. What we can do is to look at various clues which suggest that this abuse is widespread, and infinitely more common than official statistics indicate and that, in Forward's words, 'the traditional estimate of one in a million is no more than a wish'.

The first clue lies in what is already known about sex crimes in general. It is now recognised that these are seriously under-reported, as Rape Crisis Centres have been able to demonstrate, with below-average prosecution and conviction rates. Various studies have suggested that up to 50 per cent of sex crimes go unreported. Florence Rush neatly sums up the problems involved:

> Most sex offences are never revealed; when revealed, most are either ignored or not reported; if reported, a large percentage are dismissed for lack of proof, and when proof is established many are dropped because of the pressure and humiliation forced on the victim and family by the authorities.

These problems are likely to be especially acute in incest cases.

The second clue comes from growing realisation and concern, especially by official agencies and child protection groups, that children are not merely battered or emotionally abused, but sexually abused as well. Much of the pioneering work on this was done in the United States by organisations like the American Humane Association; in Britain, the NSPCC and RSSPCC now voice increasing concern about the frequency of child sexual abuse, and many social services departments are looking at how to incorporate it on their 'at risk' registers.

These figures include abuse by strangers and non-relatives, and they cannot tell us about adult survivors. But they do provide a context in which to explore the frequency of family abuse, and they also help to focus attention on the whole problem. At long last, it actually exists – and that's official.

The American Humane Association have estimated that 200,000 to 300,000 American female children are sexually molested every year. They have written:

> Findings (on sexual abuse) strongly point to the probability of an enormous national incidence many times larger than the reported incidence of physical abuse of children.

'In other words', concludes Forward, 'everything you've read about the battered-child epidemic amounts to only a fraction of the problem of incest.'

After carrying out a survey among professionals who had dealt with sexually abused children, Beezley Mrazek, Lynch and Bentovim (1981) reckoned that at least three in every thousand children would be referred to professionals for sexual abuse problems during their childhood. Findings from the MORI poll for Channel 4 in 1984 suggested that a million of today's children in Britain will be sexually abused by the age of 15.

Another clue to the widespread nature of incestuous abuse comes from the explosion effect of publicising it. This can uncover both past and present cases. When Hank Giaretto (of whom more later) set up his treatment programme in California, it attracted 30 families in 1971, but 600 by 1978. When police in Hennepin County, Minnesota, started recording incest statistics separately in 1972, they found 14 cases: in 1977, there were 200 cases.

Rape Crisis centres in Britain and Ireland have noticed a remarkable increase in incest-related calls in the last two or three years, largely, they believe, because the subject has been publicised, and an upsurge in calls invariably follows special media publicity. Since 1985, a majority of Dublin RCC's calls have been related to incest or child sexual abuse. About half of Strathclyde RCC's calls, and a quarter of Edinburgh's, are similar. When Anna Raeburn broached the subject in the women's magazine *Cosmopolitan* in 1980, she was inundated with hundreds of letters from women who confessed that they were incest survivors.

Another clue comes from the delayed or incidental discovery of an incest history by therapists treating women for other problems. Susan Forward describes her own involvement:

> My work with the incest trauma grew out of my (therapy) groups, because I was amazed at the number of patients who admitted during therapy sessions to having been incest victims. I have treated more than three hundred admitted incest cases in the last decade and I am sure many more had incest stories that they never found the courage to tell.

She confidently believed more than ten million Americans had been involved in incest.

The Kempes remark drily:

> A history of incest is so commonly found among adults who,

10 or 15 years later come to the attention of psychiatrists, marriage counsellors etc ... that the failure to consider the diagnosis early on is somewhat surprising.

These findings point to an urgent need for professionals and voluntary workers in certain settings to look in a routine way for a history of incestuous abuse among women and teenage girls they are working with, or who are in their care. 'High risk' settings include mental hospitals and outpatient clinics; units dealing with sexual problems; prisons, young offenders institutions, remand centres and assessment centres; and schools for maladjusted children.

A final, powerful clue to the frequency of incest comes from the experience of anyone who is researching and writing about it. In my experience, two remarkable things happen. First, people take you aside and tell you that a certain district is the greatest, or the only, hotbed of incest in the country. (One or two professionals actually intended going to these places to do research.)

Over several years I have heard from professionals and lay people, often in confidence and always on the highest authority, that incest is rife in the following places: County Antrim; rural Aberdeenshire; the Outer Hebrides; a problem area of Portsmouth; West Lothian; East Lothian; Dublin; the Fens; Greenock; two Edinburgh housing estates, and several districts of Glasgow; Leicestershire; and parts of Wales. The message is clear. Incest happens in north, south, east and west, in towns, cities, villages and hills. Incest is 'rife' everywhere.

The second remarkable thing is that nearly everyone to whom you mention your interest has a spontaneous story to tell. A teacher in a Glasgow secondary said she was convinced the majority of girls in her class had experienced incestuous abuse. A doctor's receptionist said she was suspicious about a number of injuries to young female children which she had noticed on patients' records. Residential care workers at children's homes or assessment centres commented on how many of their girls were known or suspected of having an incest history.

A contact talked at length about her experience of growing up in a small mining village, where 'everyone knew it went on but nobody spoke about it. My mother was unusual in warning me about it when I was very small'. A friend of hers from the same village only confessed her history of incestuous abuse at the age of 29.

Incest is supposed to be a tiny and remote problem: it is also supposed to be taboo. Yet as soon as you start asking about it, the wall of silence is breached by a flood of information. The remote experience of other people becomes an experience from close to home, or from inside it.

The myths of incest

A look at the facts and figures of incest has no doubt raised in readers some commonsense expectations about the views professionals might take of the problem. In this section they will be able to compare their expectations with reality, as we examine some common theories of 'expert' writers and therapists.

MR & MRS MYTH and their daughter LOLITA

DEVIANT FATHER   COLLUSIVE MOTHER   PRECOCIOUS DAUGHTER

The majority of these take the view that on balance, incest is an undesirable or damaging practice. But this opinion is by no means universal. Incest has been rationalised as a 'functional' solution to family problems, or even as a beneficial form of behaviour.

For instance, an American team of Marine Corps physicians concluded from a case-study of 1966 that incest served

to reduce family tension by preventing confrontations with the sources of tension. The preservation of the family group is the central function of incest to the group.

Likewise, Lustig saw incest as a transaction which served to protect and maintain the family where it occurred. Father-daughter incest worked as:

> a partial alleviation of the parents' pregenital dependency needs, as a defence against feelings of sexual insufficiency, as a mechanism for the daughter's revenge against the non-nurturing mother, and as a device for reducing separation anxiety....

Bender felt these liaisons satisfied instinctual drives in a setting where alliance with an omnipotent adult condones the transgression; the act offers an opportunity to test in reality an infantile fantasy whose consequences are found to be gratifying and pleasurable. Rascovsky and Rascovsky even believed that incestuous acts diminished a person's chance of psychosis, and made for a better adjustment to the external world.

These examples bring home the point that social science is not a neutral discipline, but may be used to rationalise or actively condone the behaviour it analyses.

The second general point to be made here is that the study and treatment of incest has been dominated by the professions of psychology and psychiatry. In Henderson's words 'The subject of incest occupies a crucial position in psychoanalytic theory and psychiatric practice.'

This means that the theories found within these disciplines, especially those relating to sexuality and child development have been highly influential. Secondly, it means that the whole subject of incest has been mystified for lay people. It is hard for them to join in the debate or even understand much of the literature, which seems to proclaim: 'This is what incest is about, it is very complex but we have it sussed out and there is no point in non-professionals challenging it.'

However, the lack of training most psychologists and psychiatrists have in social science and its research methods has never seemed to inhibit them from attempting sociological studies of people who commit incest.

We can now look at the prevalent myths as they relate to children, mothers and fathers.

THE GIRLS

Fantasy theory

Myth: incest never happened

'She's been spinning everyone a tale.'

One common reaction among researchers, therapists and other professionals has been denial and disbelief. The claims and confessions of incest victims have been dismissed as fantasy.

Of course this view is often taken towards general sex crimes against women. Females are said to fantasise continually about being raped, while teenage girls' accounts of molestation by teachers or youth club leaders are dismissed as wishful thinking based on a 'crush'. But the fantasy view of incest has particularly tenacious roots in psychological theory. The crucial role belongs to Freud, who is unlikely to win any medals for his services to women.

Freud was struck by the sheer number of his female patients who claimed to have suffered incestuous abuse. He originally theorised that childhood molestation was a trauma faced by all his hysterical patients, and was a cause of their disorder.

But he found their accounts of respectable middle-class family life increasingly hard to believe, as he makes clear in his letter to Wilhelm Fliess in 1897.

> Then there was the astonishing thing that in every case blame was laid on perverse acts by the father ... though it was hardly credible that perverted acts against children were so general.

Instead of investigating the possible truth of these accounts, Freud applied a kind of upside-down logic. Because he could not believe them, he decided they were really memories of fantasy. This belief led him to develop his theories of infantile sexuality, where universal incestuous fantasies crystallised in the Oedipus Complex. So he replaced the notion of actual trauma with the idea that these memories represented a failure to set aside incestuous fantasies and wishes.

Freud's followers continued this assumption, and made the child's desire and fantasy the basis of psychological inquiry. The adult's desire, and his capacity for active initiation, were forgotten.

In his discussion of orality in the hysterical personality, Marmor gives us an example of the webs that theorists have woven. He notes that:

> the incestuous dream of the hysteric may reflect not so much the symbolic wish to cohabit with the parent but rather a deeper pregenital wish to be loved and protected by the mother, to the exclusion of the world. The hysteric is approached as a woman but wishes to be taken as a child.

Thus after Freud, many clinicians began dismissing their patients' reports of incestuous abuse as fantasy. This has caused disquiet, even within their own profession.

Ferenczi's doubts came from hearing the confessions of adult men about their sexual involvement with children. Other writers have suggested that dismissal can be destructive, driving patients out of treatment or into psychosis by the denial of what they know to be reality.

Likewise the clinician at the Center for Rape Concern in Philadelphia has said:

> My own experience, both in private practice and with several hundred child victims brought to us, has convinced me that analysts too often dismissed as fantasy what was the real sexual molestation of a child ... as a result the victim was isolated and her trauma compounded.

But despite this concern the fantasy view persists among some clinicians. It has also become part of the folk wisdom of other agencies.

For example policemen, social workers and residential care staff will repeatedly remark how often teenage girls who run away from home claim to be victims of incestuous abuse. But many are at pains to point out the problems these claims present. 'You see, she could be spinning us a yarn as an excuse'; 'It's well known they often say that out of spite to get back at their parents', etc. The great majority of runaways are simply returned to their homes by the authorities.

We can only guess how momentous might have been the consequences for several generations of incest survivors if Freud had stuck to his original theory, and if his followers had searched actively for an incest history in disturbed patients, from the belief that it was a major cause of mental disorder. This, of course, is just the belief that puzzled therapists, looking at the accumulation of incest histories on their records, are now increasingly turning to after almost a century of denial.

The consequences for incest victims of theories about childhood sexuality, which Freud developed from his 'fantasy' notion, have been more momentous still.

Child collusion or victim blame theories

One result of beliefs that children invite, enjoy or culturally accept incest has been non-intervention by professional agencies. Those who are abused have also been given the sense that professionals they do consult blame them for their childhood experiences. This has compounded their guilt and confusion.

The concept of 'victim precipitation' grew fashionable in the 1960's and 1970's, especially in social science writing about sex crimes and other crimes against females like wife-battering. The popular myth that 'she must have asked for it' was given intellectual credibility, especially by psychology, which has been strongly anti-feminist in theory and practice. But people who think themselves liberal and progressive, who would be most upset at being called anti-feminist or anti-children, have also contributed to a climate of opinion where the whole issue of children's vulnerability to exploitation is minimised.

Myth: children are very sexy

'You have to understand the dynamics of childhood sexuality/

children are very sexy, you know/some of these girls are very precocious and may initiate the whole thing.'

Let us consider first the thinking of those nice, educated people. Freud said children were sexual beings, however hotly reactionaries like Mrs Whitehouse might protest at the idea. We must not be shocked nor puritanical, but allow kids, within reason, to express their sexuality. We must also accept that children have minds of their own, with the ability to choose.

Penal reformers are also understandably concerned at hysterical, vindictive public attitudes to sex offenders against children. In their search for a more rational, productive approach to treatment, they find very attractive any 'evidence' which minimises damage done by the crime, and points to the harmlessness of the offender.

Thus in their 1976 Submission on sexual offences, the NCCL quote with approval a string of researchers who play down damage to child victims, and stress Virkunnen's findings in a study of 64 paedophiles, 'Aggressive behaviour was not as a rule characteristic … they seemed to be in a pronounced manner gentle, fond of children and benevolent.'

Implicit in the views we have mentioned is an optimistic view of human relationships, which derives, one suspects, from the sheltered upbringing of many educated liberals. They draw on a world free of serious exploitation and sordid experience, where sex is linked with loving relationships or with free decisions to pursue one's pleasure. This kind of optimistic (some would say irresponsibly naive) thinking pervades the NCCL document.

The general theme of 'victim precipitation' in sex crimes against children has been popularised by writers like Leroy Schultz. In one paper he opens with the phrases so often heard from social workers and psychiatrists, 'Both offender and victim are symbiotic, or form a co-operative dyad.'

Stressing the affection-seeking behaviour of many child victims, he discusses other researchers' categorisations of such children, e.g. 'collaborative', 'non-objecting', 'seducing', 'fully participating', etc. When discussing ways of making legal proceedings less traumatic, he is at pains to minimise the mental and physical damage done by assaults, though his claims here conflict with the findings of de Francis' major study.

Lo and behold, in Dobash and Dobash we discover the same Leroy Schultz has researched wife-beating. In his attempt to find the 'common dynamic core' of the assaults he studied, he began with the statement:

> The victims in spouse assaults can always be assumed to have played a crucial role in the offense, and may have directly or indirectly brought about or precipitated their own victimisation.

Perhaps the most famous quote on child participation in sex crimes comes from Bender and Blau:

> These children undoubtedly do not deserve completely the cloak of innocence with which they have been endowed by moralists, social reformers and legislators ... in some cases the child assumed an active role in initiating the relationship ... it is true that the child often rationalised with excuses of fear of physical harm or the enticement of gifts, but there were obviously secondary reasons ... these children were distinguished as unusually charming and attractive in their outward personalities. Thus ... we have frequently considered the possibility that the child might have been the actual seducer, rather than the one innocently seduced.

In his review of the incest literature, Henderson notes a major finding, 'Incestuous daughters are generally felt to encourage their fathers' sexual advances, or at least to refrain from discouraging them.'

The idea that children may actually seduce or 'encourage' their fathers has its main source in the Freudian theory that all children go through a phase of incestuous desire for their parents, and that the sexuality of children is developed at an early age.

These beliefs have strongly influenced the clinical practice of psychologists and psychiatrists who treat disturbed children. At an Edinburgh incest seminar, attended by various representatives of the 'caring professions' two child psychiatrists from a major hospital protested when members of the audience talked about the exploitation of vulnerable children:

> A great deal of clinical practice suggests kids from 2–3 years have strong desires of an incestuous nature ... interviewing them, they know what sex is, they understand....

> Active steps are taken to maintain and initiate sex relationships with adults ... children are very sexy and at times may choose to be ... the commonness of incest may come back to the sexiness of children.

Thus too the NCCL writers stress 'Contemporary psychological research has shown that children have sexual feelings and desires from a very early age.'

These desires may be conscious or unconscious, so there is no way that children who deny collusion can win the argument. Sloane and Karpinski make the point: 'The "traumatic" aspect (of incest) loses some of its significance when it is realised that the child itself often unconsciously desires the sexual activity and becomes a more or less willing partner in the act.'

The literature abounds with argument that the girl's initial involvement sprang from a range of oedipal desires and conflicts. We can select Rascovsky and Rascovsky, who are using a 'Kleinian theoretical framework', to illustrate the extremes to which this convoluted thinking can go.

> Attempts at restoration from the basic depressive position (lead) to a precocious transition to the oral search for a father. In a situation dominated by extreme anxiety, there occurs an overevaluation of the father's penis. The aggressive component against the partial object seeks satisfaction in the form of an urge to castrate. The incorporation of the penis as a substitute for the primary relation with the mother's breast leads her to a masculine identification with the penis, and there follows the choice of a feminine object disguised as a womanly man. The

nymphomania results from anxiety over failure to obtain an orgasm, and the ego develops a greater capacity for sublimation favoured by the real satisfaction afforded by incest.

What is wrong with these theories of child collusion?

We can note first that in the great majority of crimes, nobody thinks of blaming the victim. People who are mugged are not accused of collusion, while in child-battering cases, society's wrath falls on the parents. Secondly, in most areas of life, especially in the area of legal rights, children are not regarded as people who know their own minds and make free choices. They are expected to do what they are told by those in authority, especially their parents.

The major problem is that child collusion theories can only be maintained by large-scale denial of people's own accounts of their first incestuous experiences.

Many writers seem content to theorise without recording or requesting the victims' memories of the event. But we can still find a good number of accounts, and they bear striking resemblances to each other. One example was given at the start of this book: we can select two others and compare them with the Kleinian explanation of Rascovsky and Rascovsky. First Noreen Winchester's statement to her solicitor.

When I was 11 my father was drunk and my mother was in hospital ... I was following my sister to go to bed when he pulled me by the arm and got me into his bedroom and ripped the dress I had on. I started crying and scared and he pushed me into bed and got on top of me and had intercourse for a long period and it was very sore. I did not know what to do so when he had fallen asleep I sneaked out and cried till I went to sleep ... I was so entirely frightened of him the way he went on, he was that sort of a person that you would have to do what he told ...

Secondly from an interview with Sweetman

The whole incestuous thing began when I was about three and a half. In the mornings when mammy went downstairs I used to get into their bed, I wanted to be cuddled. It would start off as affection, tickling, then it would turn bad, violent ... when I was eight my father raped me. It was evening. I was in bed and he came in. He started walking slowly towards me ... all I can remember is him being over me, pinning my arms down on either side of me so I couldn't move, his penis was out – after that I just blanked out ... it's like an accident; when the physical pain becomes too much you go unconscious. After that I became terrified of being in the bedroom.

From these and other accounts, several points emerge repeatedly: active initiation by the father; his use of force or authority to gain compliance; the girl's ignorance about sex, and her confusion about what is happening; her shame, fear or terror; and lack of pleasure in the painful act.

Oedipal theories take no account of the enormous gap in power and authority between parent and child. Given the child's physical development, they also appear to argue for masochism in young children. The third gap, in knowledge and understanding about sex, they deny altogether.

Yet even if survivors' consistent claims of sexual ignorance fail to convince them, they have to face some critical questions about the whole theory of infantile sexuality.

The contribution Freud made to psychological understanding, and his many insights, are not in question. He was a pioneer in the attempt to understand links between biology, environment and psychology, and to relate sexuality to the rest of personality. But he was not infallible, especially in his claims about the female sex. His theory of clitoral-vaginal transference is long discredited; his notion of penis envy has faced comprehensive professional criticism, and most women today would find it so arrogant and absurd as to be laughable. The crucial role of social gender-learning as opposed to innate drives in shaping sexuality has also been recognised by many writers, though most research on incest seems to take no account of expert criticism of Freudian theories. So it is quite possible that Freud was simply wrong about childhood incestuous fantasies too, especially when we recall the highly dubious starting-point for the theory, his refusal to believe patients' accounts of childhood abuse. And if he was wrong, the whole edifice supporting years of clinical practice towards incest victims simply collapses.

This is not to deny that young children feel strong needs for physical and emotional reassurance from parents; that their feelings towards parents are often strong, often ambivalent, and marked by emotions from jealousy to possessiveness to confusion. What is highly questionable is the validity of linking all these emotions and needs directly to oedipal fantasies and wishes.

Likewise we need not retreat into a reactionary position to question more general aspects of Freud's views on infant sexuality. We can accept that children are not some separate, neuter category of humanity but are at least latently sexual beings, capable of sensual feeling and enjoyment. But this does not mean they understand their own gestures and behaviour in the same way that adults do, nor that they see any sexual meaning in the messages they send out to others. Nor does acknowledgement that children are sexual beings imply that they are either physically or emotionally ready and able to participate in a sexual relationship. Least of all does it mean they have given permission to be exploited and abused.

Stevia Jackson argues that Freudians who interpret a wide range of infant and child behaviour as inherently sexual have mistakenly imposed the language of adult sexual experience on the behaviour of children. They have imputed sexual motives solely on the basis of the meaning those actions would have for an adult. But it is not till puberty that the child accepts itself as a sexual actor and learns the socio-sexual scripts that are expected of 'normal' adolescents and adults.

When adults say children are very sexy, what they mean is that adults including child psychiatrists find them sexy. They choose to interpret enticing smiles and affectionate physical contact as signs of sexual interest and invitation. But young children, who are even more self-centred than adults, quickly learn that charm can win them favours children want: sweets, presents, forgiveness for bad behaviour. They become adept at playing parents and relatives off against each other, 'winding Daddy round their little finger', etc., because it gets them things they both desire and understand. Little girls are positively encouraged to behave in this 'winsome' way, to act 'the charming little miss' and 'please Daddy'. Their reward is to be accused of seduction or collusion when they are sexually exploited.

The biggest giveaway in adult claims about child sexual desires is found in the enticements adult sex abusers, from incestuous fathers to the stereotyped paedophiles in playgrounds, actually offer their victims.

If children really did share the sexual desires and feelings of adults, if they could understand and take part as equals in a sexual relationship, they would respond to the overtures and 'courtship gestures' adults use on one another. But adult seducers betray their own awareness of the child's lack of understanding, either by resorting to coercion, or by holding out favours they know children want: sweets, money, a car ride in the country.

A final point needs to be made here. Placing responsibility on the male adult is not the same as demanding that he be lynched, castrated or given a life sentence. There are plenty of sound arguments for imposing constructive penalties on offenders. But any case should not be built at the victim's cost, either by blaming her, or belittling her trauma and suffering. In any case, the main problem is not what to do about the tiny minority of offenders who are caught: it is how to halt the behaviour of that vast majority who are not.

Nothing has been more influential in convincing researchers and professional agencies that girls must have invited, enjoyed or accepted incest than the long duration of most incestuous relationships. Length of time 'proves' compliance. We find many comments like this eg. from Weiner:

> The length and frequency of these incestuous contacts and the absence of any complaints on the part of the daughters indicates that these girls were not merely helpless victims of their father's needs, but were gratified by the relationship.

Myth: incest is an accepted part of some sub-cultures

> 'It is a way of life in some families, you know. They just seem to accept it and don't feel horrified like we would.'

The search for answers about why girls might accept these relationships for so long has produced a second popular myth of incest: the subculture theory.

The subculture theory has been perhaps the greatest cause, and justification, of inaction among caring agencies where incest cases are known or suspected. It was given intellectual respectability by Lukianowicz, who found that the families of most girls in her sample were of low social status.

> One might hypothesise that (the fathers') incestuous activity was (rather) the expression of a type of sexual behaviour accepted by the subculture of their social groups ... such interpretation seems to be supported by the fact that most of the girls accepted their fathers' sexual behaviour as 'normal' ... a further confirmation of our hypothesis might be found in the unusually condoning attitude on the part of the mothers.

Lukianowicz' case reports also have throwaway lines like 'everybody seems to be quite happy in this rather unusual household'.

Thus I was told by one of Noreen Winchester's caseworkers, 'It's part of their subculture. They don't look on it in the same way as you or I.' A social worker in a large Edinburgh housing estate told a Women's Aid volunteer that incest was 'a normative part of the subculture here' and 'best left alone'. A social worker anxiously told an Edinburgh seminar I attended about one of her cases, 'She (the victim) accepted the relationship, and thought there wasn't much wrong till she went out to work.'

What are the main faults of culture theories?

First, we have already shown that incest is by no means confined to 'problem families' or the lower working class (for whom the euphemism 'subculture' stands). Biased sampling methods, and the fact that they are more likely to come to the attention of caring agencies, have led to their over-representation in the incest statistics.

Secondly, culture theorists are guilty of a major fallacy. They assume that what is acceptable to the person who benefits from abuse is also acceptable to the victim. But because an exploiter finds something enjoyable and convenient, this in no way means the exploited will do likewise.

Throughout history, those who benefited from abuses or were content to tolerate them have always claimed the victims really wanted things this way: that therefore there was no exploitation. Different generations have been told that slaves were quite happy; that native 'boys' really wanted the firm adult guidance of colonial masters; that the poor did not want good housing, for they would only keep coal in the bath. Dobash and Dobash remind us of a familiar modern argument in these extracts from evidence submitted to the Parliamentary select committee on marital violence in 1975. A Catholic marriage adviser said, 'It would appear that in some groups of people violence is a normal part of the character of life, and that their tolerance towards it may be high'. A principal social worker said, 'There has been a history of violence though within that history the family ... may exist quite happily in this situation ... it is accepted as part of (the marriage) that there should be occasional assaults'.

Dobash and Dobash point out, 'These views reveal either a considerable insensitivity to, or an ignorance of, the woman's evaluation of her marriage, the violence, and her predicament'.

Likewise, theorists of an 'incest culture' can only maintain their position by denying or ignoring the survivors' accounts. Their ability to do this can be remarkable. For instance, certain legal and social work professionals in the Noreen Winchester case stuck to their view that 'she didn't mind' or 'it was part of her culture' despite the existence of a statement to her lawyers soon after arrest which even the hardened lay reader would find harrowing.

It is difficult to understand how anyone could interpret the straightforward account of her family life, including rapes, constant beatings and financial deprivation that meant continual hunger for the children, as a sign that she accepted or enjoyed her experiences.

Often, of course, professionals do not even give themselves the chance to hear and judge the survivor's account because their culture theory has dissuaded them from intervening at all. Dobash and Dobash neatly point out the self-fulfilling prophecies of non-intervention in family violence:

> The ill-conceived belief that the woman considers the violence to be normal or acceptable may lead the worker to treat the case in an unproductive manner, that is not oriented towards either eliminating the violence or helping the woman escape from it. The result of these beliefs and inaction is that the woman's position remains unchanged, which confirms the caseworker's belief that (she) considers the violence to be normal and acceptable, and does not truly want it to end. . . .

Another problem for the culture theorists is that they tie themselves in terrible knots. They are usually trying to show that the girl took on the mores of her neighbourhood. As Sloane and Karpinski sternly tell us. 'The segment of the community in which these girls lived was notorious for its sexual laxity.'

But many writers are simultaneously trying to prove that isolation from the rest of the community contributed to incest. Sloane and Karpinski's girls lived in rural Pennsylvania, and we all know what goes on in isolated farmsteads. 'All our six farmers and eleven farm labourers lived a lonely life on remote farms, without any social contacts or amenities' confesses Lukianowicz. They also have to face the fact that many incestuous fathers deliberately isolate their families from social contact.

The problem of having to prove that contamination by neighbourhood mores and lack of contamination encourage incest has led to lame and contradictory conclusions. For instance, Sloane and Karpinski think factors promoting the breakdown of the incest barrier may include, 'the lowering of social consciousness which results from the prevailing moral laxity of the community, the absence of association with the rest of the community'.

Perhaps the biggest failing of the culture theorists is their lack of imagination about why girls might endure incest in silence for many years. Their theory comes into the category of 'it must have been that, because I can't think of any other reason'. This mental block exists about each phase of the incestuous relationship.

In the early years, many victims may simply not understand what is happening; and their fathers, good 'culture theorists', will often tell them this is something all normal fathers and daughters do. Society's taboo on discussing incest is also strongest where young children are concerned. Thus the children's other contacts, like primary school teachers, are hardly likely to raise the subject or ask searching questions.

Noreen Winchester confessed that she did not really understand what was happening till she began secondary school, and heard other girls talking about sex. Likewise Mary (quoted in Stucker) explained, 'You just never heard about incest. And my dad and I never talked about what was going on. It was just something he did and left.'

She also described how it seemed impossible to resist her father.

'I can remember hitting him a few times, but most of the time I would just feel powerless and cry. I'd just lie there and hope it would hurry and be over.'

These feelings of powerlessness are likely to be strongest in the pre-pubertal years. In Ferenczi's words, 'The overwhelming force and authority of the adult makes them numb and can rob them of their senses'.

If children turn to anyone at this stage for help and protection, it is most likely to be their mothers. But for reasons we shall discuss later, many mothers do not, or cannot, intervene effectively to protect their children.

When the girl eventually does realise what is going on, a host of problems may still prevent her reporting it to anyone.

Case reports show that shock, anger, guilt and disgust usually follow understanding of the act, and of society's strong moral condemnation. This often produces new efforts to end the liaison and to more open coercion or threats by the father. The very feelings that make girls want to end the incest also prevent them seeking the help they need. Shame and humiliation only strengthen the taboo on discussion: girls feel alienated from their peers, stigmatised and abnormal.

'I could never have told my closest friend: I felt bad and dirty all the time,' said Noreen Winchester. Her siblings felt similarly ashamed, and one even tried to change her surname after the court case. Mary said 'I had no close friends in school. If I had gotten close to people, the incest would have come out. I always felt dirty: my whole body felt dirty to me.'

Thus girls seem to share researchers' opinions about themselves. They feel they must somehow be to blame, all the more so if they have sometimes enjoyed the incestuous act. This leads to the belief that they do not deserve help, but punishment: that what they have started, they must continue to endure.

Even if they do think of telling someone or escaping, they usually do not know where to seek help. Many working class families, especially, lack the knowledge or the confidence to help them find a source of support: many teenagers are even nervous of using the telephone. They also lack the economic means to set up on their own, and as we have noted, most runaways are simply returned to their families.

That social agencies still remain oblivious to these obvious problems of 'know-how' has already been shown in their familiar response to wife-beating, 'Surely she could have left?' 'Why didn't she complain, then?' This mental block is still more puzzling when we consider that most caring agencies themselves openly admit that they do not know how on earth to help incest victims. If this is so, it is hardly surprising that the girls do not know where to turn, or lack confidence in existing agencies.

Even when girls seriously contemplate exposing the situation, they become aware that this will probably break up the home. Recriminations, publicity, social ostracism, imprisonment and loss of breadwinner, and removal into care are likely to follow. In the Kempes words, 'If she ends (the relationship) ... she will forfeit the family security that, she believes, her compliance has assured her, her mother and her siblings. This is a terrible burden for these immature women to carry.

So it is hardly surprising if some shrink from it, especially when they calculate realistically their chances of support. For the Kempes point out a regular finding, 'In order to preserve the family, the members often deny the incest even after it has been discovered and tend to condemn the victim if she is the cause of the discovery.'

Relatives who initially pledge support may back down and accuse the girl of inventing the whole story. Saddest of all, as Forward notes and illustrates with case histories, admission may lead other male relatives like uncles to take further sexual advantage of the incest victim.

Much of the process we have described in this section has been clarified very usefully by Roland Summit in his work on the 'accommodation syndrome', which should be on the reading list of anyone dealing with cases of incestuous abuse.

He identifies five stages, all of which conspire to prevent exposure and force children to endure years of abuse, whatever their cultural background. First there is secrecy, which is both the source of fear and the promise of safety, 'Everything will be all right if you just don't tell'.

Then there is helplessness, the lack of power to protest or say no. Children do not call on force to deal with overwhelming threat or confusion. Trusted adults define a child's reality and when there is no place to run they have no choice but to try and hide. The threat of loss of love or security involved in protesting may be more frightening to a child than the threat of violence.

Then there is entrapment and accommodation. To make sense of the abuse, children grow to believe they must have provoked or deserved the assaults, and anger is most likely to be translated into self-destructive behaviour. Anyone working with the child may be tested and provoked to prove that trust is impossible: it is all too easy to join the parent and adult society in rejecting such a child.

Then there is delayed, conflicting or unconvincing disclosure. If the girl is driven to let go the secret, she seeks understanding and intervention just when she is least likely to find them, when people are alienated by her delinquency and rebellious anger, and assume she has invented the story in retaliation. An adolescent already branded a troublemaker and ungrateful child risks not just disbelief but humiliation and punishment too.

In that situation the next stage, retraction, is an easy response to pressure. The child bears the responsibility of preserving or destroying the family. The 'bad' choice is to tell the truth, the 'good' choice is to capitulate, restore the lie and save the family. And the likely response, spoken or unspoken, from the family, the public and social agencies when she restores the lie is, 'Now then, that's better'. This merely confirms the child's belief that no one can help, and confirms adult expectations that children cannot be trusted.

The final problem, of course, is that even when girls do report they are frequently disbelieved by professionals, especially if they have fallen into the familiar pattern of drug abuse or promiscuity, and do not appear as 'credible witnesses'.

Myth: incest reflects a caring relationship

'It could be a deeply caring relationship. We don't want to take a blanket view and disrupt something meaningful.'

A child psychiatrist at the Edinburgh incest seminar asked, 'But suppose they had a warm, loving, caring relationship?' Again, during the Noreen Winchester case, I was repeatedly told by social workers and lawyers that Noreen 'really' loved her father! Schultz has much to say in support of these views

> Incest cases pose a special problem in that a girl victim *(sic)* may have developed a strong affection for her father over a long period of time. Courts and social agencies are quick to separate the family members, with little preparation for the child's loss of the source of her affection.

The first problem about all this is that people who express such views are very often the same people who believe relationships in incestuous families are seriously impaired or distorted. It is widely held, especially among social workers, that incest is only a symptom of family disorganisation, that a host of personal failings and problems produce a lack of proper parenting and caring. Alcoholism, mental illness, inadequacy, psychopathy and low morals (loveless, promiscuous, sexual relationships) among fathers, mothers and daughters are frequently invoked as a cause of this disorganisation and its results. The very people who are said to be incapable of warm, loving, responsible, caring relationships, or of meaningful sexual intimacy, are then said to be expressing precisely these things through incest!

If we are to accept research findings that many survivors experience unhappy home lives, lack of affection and other family problems, the experts cannot simultaneously expect us to believe offender and victim were merely expressing the depth of their warm feelings and mutual respect. Professionals must make up their minds just which of their contradictory theories they wish to pursue and have accepted, as a basis for professional treatment.

The second problem comes when we ask ourselves if truly caring fathers, who will be among the readers of this book, would inflict on their children the emotional turmoil of a 'caring trap' sensitively described by Herman and Hirschman.

> Susan Brownmiller ... calls (incest) father-rape. To label it thus is to understate the complexity of the relationship ... to describe what occurs as rape is to minimise the harm to the child, for what is involved here is not simply an assault, it is a betrayal. A woman who has been raped can cope with the experience in the same way that she would react to any other intentionally cruel and harmful attack. She is not socially or psychologically dependent on the rapist. She is free to hate him. But the daughter who has been molested is dependent on her father for protection and care. She has no recourse. She does not dare express, or even feel, the depths of her anger at being used. She must comply with her father's demands or risk losing the parental love that she needs ... she must endure it, and find in it what compensation she can.

The third problem arises over how we interpret research findings that many girls express ambivalent and even warm feelings towards their fathers. For instance Herman and Hirschman's subjects described their fathers much more favourably than their mothers, and seemed more willing to forgive them. These positive comments have lent weight to the theory that girls commit incest because they are in love with their fathers or share a close, loving relationship.

But this view ignores the complexities of emotion involved, and mistakes effect for cause. Ambivalence can be seen as the result of the incest situation, where the girl seeks 'coping mechanisms' to make her situation bearable. It may also result from sexist assumptions about family roles and duties, which are shared by all members of the family, and indeed by professional agencies.

Pleasure in the sexual act can produce ambivalence, though it should be stressed that 'freezing up' appears much more common. Thus Lenore, in Herman and Hirschman, explained, 'The whole issue is very complicated. I was very attracted to my father, and that just compounded the guilt.'

This feeling makes survivors much more reluctant to condemn their fathers, and increases their own sense of blame for complicity in the incest.

Another reason for mixed feelings is that the relationship has often given girls some semblance of affection, status and power, the only kind they have received. These are some compensation for a plight from which they cannot escape. We can quote again from Herman and Hirschman.

> These were men whose presentation to the outside world made them liked and often respected members of the community. The daughters responded to their fathers' social status and power and derived satisfaction from being their fathers' favourites. They were 'daddy's special girls', and often they were special to no one else. Feelings of pity for the fathers were also common, especially where the fathers had lost social status (as a result of exposure).
>
> Although the victims reported that they felt helpless and powerless against their fathers, the incestuous relationship did give them some semblance of power within the family. Many ... effectively replaced their mothers and became their fathers' surrogate wives ... and were generally given some authority over (the younger children) ... they did gain some feeling of value and importance from the role they were given. Many girls felt an enormous sense of responsibility for holding the family together.

Thus Noreen Winchester was the eldest of a family of eight, and for long periods had the main responsibility for feeding and caring for the other children. This was one reason why she felt it would have been impossible to leave. Finally:

> They also knew that, as keepers of the incest secret, they had an extraordinary power to destroy the family. (The incest) conferred on them a sense of possessing a dangerous, secret power over the lives of others, which they derived from no other source ... keeping up appearances and doing whatever was necessary to maintain the integrity of the family became a necessary, expiating act at the same time as it increased the daughters' sense of isolation and shame.

Women are bound to feel confused and ambivalent about fathers who have given them positive roles and feelings, as well as negative ones. But whether professionals should see the former as beneficial, as proof that incest 'did girls no harm', is another matter. There is nothing very positive about compensations which destroy or pervert a person's self-image. For instance, the 'secret sense of power' has encouraged victims to believe themselves evil and wicked: witches, whores and 'devil's children'.

Perhaps the most striking thing about survivors' comments is their implicit acceptance of traditional beliefs about men and women, and family roles. Why did they keep excusing and forgiving their fathers, blaming their mothers and themselves? They would seem to have accepted a string of patriarchal notions about the family, described by Herman and Hirschman:

> Customarily, a mother and wife in our society is one who nurtures and takes care of children and husband. If . . . the mother is unable to fulfil her ordinary functions, it is apparently assumed that some other female must be found to do it. The eldest daughter is a frequent choice. (When the wife is incapacitated) he feels his first right is to continue to receive the services his wife formerly provided, sometimes including sexual services. This view of the father's prerogative to be served not only is shared by the fathers and daughters in these families, but is also encouraged by societal attitudes. . . .

Thus we find 'Theresa' saying 'I used to think that my father was really yelling at my mother because she wouldn't give him sex. I felt I had to make it up to him.'

'Mrs V', quoted by Lukianowicz, says of her father 'I think it was quite natural for him to do so after his wife left him.'

Not all victims would feel their responsibilities went as far as that. But most do not seem to expect their fathers to endure prolonged sexual abstinence, nor to take on a maternal caring role if the mother is incapacitated or leaves. Most important and revealing, they do not expect their fathers to protect them, so when they fail to do so, their excesses can be understood and pitied, if not forgiven.

It is mothers whom the girls very strongly expect to protect their children. Their enormous sense of betrayal can only be understood in the context of this deep rooted belief. They feel mothers have not only failed to satisfy their husbands' needs: they have failed in their most basic duty to protect young and vulnerable children. Their views have been echoed by researchers and therapists, for example Tormes actually says 'the mother is the only possible agent of incest control within the family group'. As researchers pile blame on incest offenders' wives, so the victims do likewise.

Myth: the incest victim is a bad sort of girl anyway

'Well, her behaviour does seem to indicate that she is a certain sort of girl. There's no getting away from it.'

Here the behaviour of the teenager or adult woman outside the incestuous relationship, or after it has been ended, is used to suggest that her basic morals and character made her invite, enjoy or accept incest. The starting-point is that many abused girls indulge in promiscuous sexual behaviour, especially with older men. Others turn to prostitution, drug abuse, petty crime and other forms of anti-social behaviour.

By seeing these activities as the cause, rather than the effect, of incestuous abuse, experts can minimise or deny the damage done by incest. The girls' credibility is also further undermined. The accounts and feelings of such 'bad girls' must be taken with more than a pinch of salt, and their treatment and future must be put in the hands of responsible people.

We can quote Lukianowicz for an example of the 'back side forwards' argument.

Our impression was that the girls in whom the frequency of (incestuous) intercourse was high belong to two groups: those who later became promiscuous, and to those who did not show any ill effects ... if this observation was correct, one might assume that (their) participation in the incestuous activities ... was not entirely passive.

Promiscuous behaviour can be used to bolster 'culture theories'. It further 'proves' that the incest victim merely learned and accepted lax or deviant home morals. The way these girls 'turned out' later brings a sad and knowing shake of the head. How can one change these cultures, or give the youngsters a proper sense of right and wrong?

Sloane and Karpinski's girls, we recall, came from a segment of the community 'notorious for its sexual laxity'. Promiscuity among married and unmarried people was the rule. The household of promiscuous Carrie, 'a clear-cut delinquent with an attitude of brazen defiance' was unbelievably distasteful to the researchers.

The maternal grandmother, still alive, was reputed to have

extremely low morals ... the family consisted of five children, all of low mentality ... some idea of the moral status of the home can be obtained from the fact that Carrie had no hesitation in relating her sexual experiences in detail to her mother.

This class prejudice, which reaches an almost vicious level in these authors, is common in the research literature.

Incest survivors' tendency towards promiscuity with older partners is also used to hint or 'prove' that the girls actively sought a relationship with their fathers, and gained gratification from it. Now they are seeking substitutes to compensate for the lost father etc. Running through the Lukianowicz examples below is the assumption that promiscuity fulfilled some sexual need in the girl.

> In almost all cases of a later promiscuity the girls concerned actively chose adult males ... in preference to adolescents. This behaviour might further suggest that at least some of the girls concerned might have played an active part in the initiation of the incestuous relations.

The main objection to such retrospective theories is simply that no self-respecting social researcher should use them. There is no accurate way of knowing what someone's character and behaviour would have been like if a major part of their life experience (here, incestuous abuse) had never happened. To say, 'Ah, the way she behaves at fifteen explains what she did at seven', is to deny the influence, even the reality, of what happened in the years between. (It also turns on its head the usual thinking of psychiatrists and social workers, some of whom take to obsessive lengths their training-rules that explanations of adult behaviour are found in early childhood experience!)

Secondly, these theories, like so many others discussed here, can only be maintained if the experts ignore evidence in front of their noses.

Though a history of promiscuity is often found we find still more often a revulsion against sex. One of Lukianowicz's subjects made a typical comment, 'I hate sexual intercourse. I get stiff with fear when anyone approaches me with sex. I can't stand it anymore.'

Further, many women show both kinds of behaviour: 'promiscuity' and 'frigidity'.

Clearly then we need an explanation that can square these two contradictory findings. 'She just wants sex' cannot do this. The idea that promiscuity reflects sexual cravings simply will not do unless we ignore the 'frigidity' findings.

The idea that prostitution has anything to do with sexual needs or enjoyment would be challenged by many different theorists on the topic, from functionalists to radicals, and indeed by prostitutes themselves. There is also strong evidence that promiscuous relationships have little to do with sexual desires, a great deal to do with the psychological damage suffered.

First there's that jargon word 'socialisation'. The girl's behaviour may simply reflect the expectations that incest has taught her. In Weber's words 'many of the victims ... strongly believe that the only thing any man is after is sex, and that all they (the victims) are good for is sex.'

Nor is this surprising if, when she carries these expectations into new relationships outside the family, she also tends to choose partners much older than herself. This is the only kind of relationship of which she has any experience, and often the offender has actively tried to isolate her from normal peer group contacts until her mid or even late teens. They form a strange and unfamiliar world. As we have seen, the girl may further isolate herself from peer group contacts at school and work, because she feels 'dirty' and stigmatised.

Secondly, promiscuous contacts can reflect an inability to make stable relationships and/or a desperate search, continually unsuccessful, to get close to somebody else. Why might survivors have problems like this?

Herman and Hirschman, among others, noted how often their patients complained that they felt isolated from other people. They could not communicate, felt 'dead inside' or worried that they were unable to love anyone. The authors linked this distancing to the device many victims used during sexual abuse, namely to shut down, to pretend it wasn't happening. 'Passive resistance and dissociation of feeling seemed to be one of the few defences available in an overwhelming situation.'

But this later carried over into other relationships in both a physical and emotional sense.

> The sense of distance and isolation which these women experienced was uniformly painful and they made repeated, often desperate efforts to overcome it. Frequently, the result was a pattern of many brief and unsatisfactory sexual contacts.

Neither unrealistic expectations, nor basic human distrust, encourage stable relationships. Herman and Hirschman reported that some victims searched for a saviour figure, an idealised protector whom of course they never found. Forward described a different but probably more common result of the incest betrayal.

'Because her first experience with trust was such a painful failure, she cannot bring herself to trust again. Her distrust alone is enough to ensure that she will not allow herself to become close to a man.'

Thirdly, and very important, promiscuous relationships reflect self-disgust and low self-esteem.

This is what the 'experts' call masochism. Masochism is the last refuge of those who are keen to prove people really enjoyed painful experiences. It is presented as some sort of inborn trait, which only women appear to possess, and it justifies official inaction by letting people blame the victim. But some writers, like Herman and Hirschman, have suggested how self-degradation may be a direct result of incestuous abuse.

Some of their sample got mixed up with men who were cruel, abusive and neglectful, while others had a string of promiscuous relationships. So did some of Forward's patients. One girl maintained a relationship with a man who had raped her.

Herman and Hirschman ask:

Why did these women feel they deserved to be beaten, raped, neglected and used? The answer lies in their image of themselves. It is only through understanding (that) that we can make sense of their often highly destructive relationships with others.

We recall that some of their subjects called themselves whores or devil's children. They had a sense of their innate evilness and one even boasted 'There's nothing I haven't done!' They also accepted the images of themselves which their parents held.

So one girl told the authors, 'I could have been the biggest bum. My father called me a big whore and my mother believed him. I could have got so disgusted I could have run around with everyone I saw.'

So they often behave in a way that confirms their self-image, and proclaims to the world, 'I'm the biggest whore around, you won't find a lower creature than me.' Forward writes of this process:

Even though she derives no pleasure from sex, her need for self-punishment as a response to her guilt may lead her to have sex with a variety of men. She may be promiscuous as a means of self-degradation, while at the same time seeking through sex the affection she never quite found in incest. Because she confuses love, guilt and sex, she ends up too often being used as a sexual object. Through her continual self-punishment she tries to cleanse herself of guilt, but her feelings won't wash away.

The feelings and problems we have discussed here suggest that many survivors need prolonged and sensitive therapy to counter the damage to their basic feelings about themselves and others. In particular, the issue of self-blame, which dominates the women's reactions for a lifetime, needs to be tackled head-on: until these women are to consider and accept that the fault lies outside themselves, they cannot build the positive future which social agencies exhort them to do, nor could they relate in a rewarding way to other people.

Incest survivor groups which have sprung up all over Britain in recent years, and which will be discussed more later in the book, have made restoration of self-respect and control a priority. While many women involved have never before been able to talk about their experiences and gain strength from each other, others have had unsatisfactory or humiliating experience of 'counselling' by those who consider themselves experts.

Even though in recent years official agencies, therapists and counselling centres have become far more willing to move away from victim blame and to emphasise the building of self-confidence, suspicion of professional methods remains strong in survivor groups. One-to-one counselling and training for workers have not been looked on enthusiastically by a number of groups. Rasjidah St John, formerly a leading member of the Incest Survivors Campaign, is one person who sees dangers in polarised positions on this issue.

Open self-help groups have many strengths, she says. But one problem is that women arrive with different needs. For some, their first anxiety is about getting specific advice, for instance on the law, or on how to tell their families about the abuse. Some will be extremely shy and find they do not have the chance to speak for several sessions which are dominated by more vocal people – and they may simply leave in disillusionment. Some may even be continuing the incestuous relationship, and this can outrage other members of the group.

She believes it is important that women have the chance of one-to-one counselling before they enter the group. The person involved does not have to be professionally trained, but they do have to be knowledgeable and sensitive. Dublin Rape Crisis Centre (discussed later) is one example of a group which uses its own trained counsellors in conjunction with self-help meetings of survivors. Perhaps this whole subject needs more open discussion and debate among Rape Crisis Centres and survivor groups, and more sharing of experience over the last few years.

Denial of damage: the consequences for intervention

We have looked at various theories which claim that girl victims initiated, accepted or enjoyed incest. The theories have been applied because they make sense to researchers: these 'starting-point' beliefs have then shaped the way they go on to interpret evidence in front of them.

If a girl enjoyed incest, for example, she could not really have been damaged, and apparent signs of harm must have other causes. So there has often been great reluctance to ascribe behaviour disorders to incestuous abuse. For instance, though Maisch found 70 per cent of girls in his study showed signs of disturbed personality development, he was still uncertain if this was the result of incest itself.

Again, Lukianowicz found only six of 26 girls seemed to suffer no ill effects. The rest showed a range of character disorders, disturbed behaviour, neuroses, and aversion to sexual relations. Yet she still clung to her subculture theory, and summed up casually 'The conclusion was arrived at that incest in girls' early life may cause in some cases personality disorders, very rarely a neurosis, never a psychosis.'

The desperate search to find other causes of harm than incest makes 'experts' pay special attention to persistent research findings that disclosure, public censure, court proceedings and family break-up cause much trauma. Some have concluded that family attitudes to incest, rather than the incest itself, are the root cause of damage. For instance Schultz warns:

> It is clear from studies of child sexual victims that it is not the sexual assault that usually creates trauma, but the child's parent's behaviour upon discovery ... in most cases sexual trauma, unless reinforced by court testifying or parental over-reaction, produces few permanent consequences.

Of course, parental hysteria may well sow undue anxiety in a child's mind if he or she has merely been 'flashed' at in a playground. But 'flashing' is very different from assault and invasion of the child's body over a long time. Pursuing the parent theme, Henderson fails to consider this difference:

Generally, if the adults involved in incestuous relations harbour little anxiety or guilt concerning the affair the daughter will do likewise... Raphling et al note that this is particularly true if the non-participating adult is permissive and allows the incestuous behaviour to be expressed in an open and forthright fashion.

Or perhaps society is at fault for insisting incest is wrong! On this view the taboo, not its violation, causes the problem. 'Apparently in our culture,' Yorukoglu muses, 'the incest taboo is so strong that when parent–child incest occurs, it is psychologically traumatic to the child involved in the act'.

But most stress has been laid on the traumatic effects of court proceedings, with their public disgrace, humiliating interrogations and effects on family unity. These experiences encourage the NCCL in their view that 'bringing in the law could do immense harm to the child'. They stress that in many cases the victim does not appear to suffer any obvious psychological disturbance till after the case has come to court.

Most important is the result of all these theories. That result is: official inaction. The findings flash a red warning signal: leave well alone, because the child would be quite all right if nobody made such a fuss, or took the case to court, or imposed their morals on a perfectly jolly subculture, etc. Anxieties about post-disclosure trauma pervade caring agencies, are voiced at every discussion group, and are used to justify past inaction. 'I stuck my neck out, I knew I was breaking the law' said one social worker proudly at the Edinburgh incest seminar. 'For her sake I didn't report it.'

The first two views we discussed namely that over-reaction by parents or society cause the damage, can only be maintained by rationalising incest as acceptable behaviour, and by massively denying all the damage it inflicts on victims.

The third belief is accurate enough: disclosure and its aftermath do bring great trauma. It is the conclusions drawn from this which are so dubious. The suffering survivors face at each stage of the disclosure process is well documented in the literature. Social workers show foresight and responsibility in worrying about how reporting will affect the child. But, of course, the answer is not for each profession to back down with a sigh: the answer lies in concerted and prolonged effort by legal, psychiatric and social work professions to find ways of making disclosure less traumatic.

Either incest is damaging and undesirable, or it is not. If professionals take the first view, they should work to surmount the barriers to having it reported and stopped: not simply collapse in front of them.

Lawyers, social workers, doctors and others should make a priority of looking at ideas that have been developed at home and abroad for easing the trauma of exposure. Some of these will be touched on in the last section of the book. They include use of tape recorded evidence, anatomically correct dolls through which young children can explain what has happened to them, and the employment of a trained adult 'advocate' who can support the child through all the procedures of a court case. The most important general need is for a speedy and co-ordinated response among different agencies.

The training of professionals in techniques and sensitivity whether by other professionals, or by voluntary workers will obviously be a vital part of developing a co-ordinated response. This should be encouraged, but it is important that those who do the training do not infringe the rights and dignity of the children they are supposed to be helping.

This can happen if, for instance, training videos are used where the child is identifiable and is shown answering a string of personal questions without her knowledge or permission. This has already happened a number of times in Britain. What must be asked is whether such videos are really necessary to training, and what their unauthorised use reveals about the attitudes of professionals who show them. You cannot treat children with partial respect. In this case, their trust has already been abused enough.

THE MOTHERS

Mother-blame theories

Myth: The collusive wife

'You see, it's a terribly complex family dynamic, and you've got to look at Mum's role in all this.'

Strong criticism from feminist writers and survivor groups has made professionals, including therapists, far more reluctant to indulge in overt 'victim blame' in the last two or three years. But the tenacious grip of 'mother-blame' theories has barely been loosened. If survivors are not to be the guilty parties, the search for responsibility far more often passes to their mothers than to the male offenders. If Lot's wife were alive today, she would be soundly berated for allowing herself to be turned into a pillar of salt.

A cynic could even say that mother-blame supports the whole edifice of family therapy in incest cases, and that many professionals have a vital stake in maintaining it, since otherwise their programmes might have a threadbare look. What underpins many of these programmes is the idea that something has gone wrong with the whole family constellation to precipitate the incestuous abuse, and that the mother must have a crucial role in this. In particular, there is a strong assumption that men have turned to incest because the marital relationship is faulty or has broken down. The fact that about one in three English marriages now ends in divorce, and that in most of these situations incest does not occur, is not discussed.

Reviewing 'victim blame' research on wife-beating. Dobash and Dobash write 'Being too talkative or too quiet, too sexual or not sexual enough, too often pregnant or not frequently enough, all seem to be provocations (to violence)'. Likewise, mothers of incest victims often seem to be caught in a catch-22 and blamed for whatever they do, for conscious and unconscious behaviour, for dependence and dominance, for promiscuity and frigidity.

We find again a striking lack of sympathetic imagination about the problems and dilemmas such mothers might face. But there is also a conspicuous lack of concern about how mothers might be supported in resolving those problems, in comparison with the time and energy spent on worrying about how offenders and survivors could be helped or treated.

Wives are often referred to as the 'silent partner'. This itself indicates that most professionals regard mothers as actual participators, conscious or unconscious, in the incest situation. Henderson sums up the accepted wisdom. 'Most authors agree that the father is aided and abetted in his incestuous liaison by a collusive wife.'

Mothers are blamed for three main faults: inadequate or flawed personalities; abandonment of wifely and motherly duties, forcing daughters into maternal roles; and by failure to take action against the incest, even though they know it is going on. They are even blamed for marrying the offender in the first place.

Summarising again, Henderson says of their personalities 'The mothers (wives) in general are found to be dependent and infantile, pathologically attached to their own mothers and prone to panic in the face of responsibility.'

Heims and Kaufman also found the mothers 'infantile persons'. Lukianowicz, interestingly enough, is unusual for presenting an ordinary picture of the mothers of her sample, in a summary that suggests faults in the husbands:

None of our mothers was psychotic, and most of them appeared to be 'normal', hard working and much suffering women, usually with large families, and either a habitually unemployed, inefficient 'good for nothing' husband ... or an aggressive and demanding husband.

Yet later she writes that eight of these mothers 'were probably psychopaths (the promiscuous mothers); two frigid women showed symptoms of hysterical personality.'

Promiscuity is an example of unwifely behaviour, and gives one explanation of why mothers might find incest to their advantage. Two of Lukianowicz' mothers had eloped with their lovers and six

were frankly promiscuous and would even bring men home when their husbands were out. So they were apparently quite happy to tolerate their husbands' 'unfaithfulness' with their own daughters, as long as their husbands did not object to their own promiscuous behaviour.

Frigidity is also unwifely, and it plays a central role in 'mother-blame' explanations.

We can quote several different authors to show the typical pattern, where wives are portrayed as deliberately (and unreasonably) forsaking their sexual duties and pushing their daughters into taking over. Henderson says 'She forces a heavy burden of responsibility on to her daughter by causing her to assume the role of wife and lover with her own father and absolving the mother of this unwanted role'. Weiner comments '(Mothers) often encourage such activity by frustrating their husbands sexually, deserting them in some fashion'. The Justices say '(She) may bow out of her role as wife, leaving the husband to look elsewhere for sex.'

One of Lustig's five conditions which foster breakdown of the incest barrier was 'the relative sexual incompatibility between the parents, leading to unrelieved sexual tension in the father.' Ebner found that in his group of 100 mothers 44, for various reasons, were not available as sexual partners.

These failures spring from the mother's general lack of wifely and motherly instincts. According to Forward:

Typically the silent partner is unable to maintain any sort of nurturing, affectionate relationship with either her husband or her daughter. This emotional abandonment of the family often causes the husband and daughter to seek emotional refuge with each other.

She goes on to describe a pattern which she admits is 'not so very different from the general disenchantment that seems to be afflicting great numbers of married women these days.' What distinguishes the silent partner is her tendency to deal with these problems by passing them on to her daughter.

(She) often pulls back from her family in an attempt to discard her emotional duties. She is often disappointed and bored with her husband ... may feel depressed that she is no longer as young and attractive as she used to be ... finding no fulfilment at home she may turn her attention elsewhere, developing new interests – volunteer work, school, a job, social commitments – as a means of escape.

'This disenchantment and resultant emotional neglect of her family' leads her unconsciously to abdicate her maternal role in a 'gradual transfer of duties that have become unpleasant to her, ranging from housekeeping to sex.'

This is, to say the least, an unsympathetic portrayal of married women's attempts to confront their problems, and their dangerous tendency to become more independent-minded. Other writers

blame mothers openly for having the nerve to go out to work, seeing this as part of a plot to force daughters into incest. The Kempes comment

Many (men), gradually sliding towards incestuous behaviour,

(sic) are given the extra push by a wife who arranges situations that allow privacy between father and daughter. She may, for example, arrange her work schedule so that it takes her away from home in the evenings, and tell her daughter to 'take care of Dad'.

Weeks comments,

> We see mothers only too happy to turn over the burdensome sexual role to their daughters, and to this end mothers take jobs that require them to be absent from the home in the late afternoon and evening hours.

The Justices even blame mothers for being exhausted. 'She keeps herself tired and worn out. This is an open invitation to the daughter to take over,' they warn us.

Like other writers, the Justices note how incest is more likely to happen when mothers are pregnant, ill in hospital, at work or chronically depressed.

Mothers' frequent failure to report incest only reinforces 'expert' views that she colluded in or encouraged the liaison. This failure is much analysed. Tormes believes:

> After examining the character of the incest family ... the unavoidable conclusion seems to be that the failure of the mother to protect the child against the contingency of incestuous victimisation is a crucial and fruitful area of study.

Professionals disagree about the proportion of mothers who wilfully 'turn a blind eye'. Forward rejects the view that all mothers participate in, or know about, incest but believes 80–90 per cent of victims' mothers do so, mainly 'on an unconscious level' Lukianowicz found that only two of the mothers of her sample reported the incest. The Kempes pass the harshest verdict:

> Stories from mothers that they 'could not be more surprised' can generally be discounted – we have simply not seen an innocent mother in long-standing incest, although the mother escapes the punishment that her husband is likely to suffer.

Henderson tells us in his review 'When these wives report the incestuous liaison it is not so much because they object to the incestuous act, but rather because they are angry over some other matter.' So mothers seem to have the choice of being collusive or spiteful.

A point needs to be made here on the whole issue of knowledge and reporting. All the signs are that the extent to which mothers have tried to take action in defence of their daughters has been seriously underestimated, and that this will become still more apparent when more mothers feel able to speak out openly about their experience.

First, we may expect that mothers have faced very similar problems to daughters in trying to persuade professionals whom they have told to take any action. Secondly, it seems that many women leave home with their children because of incestuous abuse but either they do not reveal this, or the fact is not recorded.

We have already given the example of women confessing what the 'last straw' was to workers in Women's Aid refuges. Lawyers who specialise in divorce cases have also said it is not uncommon for women to admit that incestuous abuse is the real reason why they have left home and are seeking divorce. But either they have chosen not to make the reason known publicly, or for reasons including the problems of proof, they have been advised to use other grounds. One London lawyer admitted to an incest survivors' campaigner that she had seen numerous women over many years who revealed that this was the real reason why they wanted a divorce.

Whatever the actual proportion of mothers 'turning a blind eye', it is clear from the pattern of victims' accounts that many mothers feel they cannot or should not intervene. Indeed this is a major reason for victims' intense sense of betrayal by their mothers. What explanations for this lack of action have been suggested by researchers?

We have already discussed 'abdication of role responsibility' theories, where the mother finds it a relief or a convenience to let her daughter take on wifely functions. Freudian, or pseudo Freudian, theories also raise their heads. Symbolic castration looms up in Forward's unflattering explanation of mothers' silence:

> She will often try to handle the situation without calling in the authorities, giving her the power to blackmail her husband for his misdeeds. In essence she castrates her husband and further removes herself from the maternal role.

Lukianowicz hesitantly uses subculture theory to explain mothers' unusually condoning attitude 'One may assume that the mothers also regard this relationship as an 'accepted' (though perhaps not very common and not desirable) type of behaviour in their social group.'

Additional explanations of silence put the wife's dependence in unflattering terms. Lukianowicz comments 'These women were extremely dependent on their husbands and would have allowed them to do anything they wanted for the price of remaining with them.' Kempes says 'Often a very dependent mother is frantic to hold on to her man for her own needs and the financial support he provides.'

But other writers hint at more pressing and practical reasons for the mothers' reticence. Weber suggests

Sometimes mothers are afraid of being beaten or of their family being broken up or of the loss of financial support. Often it's a vague fear of not knowing what to do, where to go, what's going to happen.

In her review of the Justices' book, Audrey Middleton points out:

If she (the mother) reports it to the social services (and if they believe her) her daughter and other vulnerable children may be taken into care. If . . . the case goes to court and there's insufficient evidence, the father will be released to vent his anger on his wife for going to the police. If the father is jailed, the mother may face economic hardship and ostracism from family, neighbours and friends.

The importance of duress comes across most forcefully in an important and pioneering paper by Dietz and Craft, who interviewed 200 American social workers about their personal experience of incestuous families. An astonishing 74 per cent said mothers in these families were likely to be victims of physical abuse by their husbands. The profiles that emerged of incestuous families were, said the authors, markedly similar to research profiles of 'wife abuse' families, with an authoritarian and domineering husband. If the wives in incestuous families faced physical violence, this would cast quite a different light on their apparent 'consent' to the incest. As the authors drily remarked, 'It is difficult to conceive how being a possible victim of physical abuse oneself makes one equally responsible with the abuser for the sexual abuse of one's child.'

Writers also note that mothers may do nothing because they simply disbelieve their daughters, or blame them for the incest.

Thus one of the Kempes' mothers

angrily denied that her husband, 'an important man in the community', would do such a thing ... she asked that he not be contacted and disowned her daughter as a chronic liar.

Forward notes that

unfortunately, most mothers react with hostility, calling their daughters home wreckers, liars, sluts.... Others become accusatory, saying 'you could have stopped it', or 'you must have wanted him to do it'.

Many incest survivors recount similar reactions by their mothers.

But these hostile reactions are not usually explained by writers, except in terms which further disparage the mother's character and motives. Forward, though, has a brief flash of 'sympathetic imagination' on this point:

She feels ... an outsider in her own home. She feels inadequate, undesired, somehow guilty ... at a time when her daughter most needs her support and understanding even the uninvolved mother may be so blinded by her own pain that she can only lash out ... the mother is jealous of her daughter, who has become 'the other woman'.

Yet at the same time she is invoking castration theories and stressing the responsibility theme:

The bulk of her anger stems from her unconscious need to deny her own responsibility. Even if she admits (that), her denial stems from an unconscious need to rationalise her involvement and displace her guilt onto her daughter.

Like other authors, Forward always seems to end up indulging in 'mother blame'.

At this point we should note a very basic, practical and human reason why any mother traditional, progressive, middle class, or working class may find it hard to believe her daughter's accusations, and face the prospect that her own husband could have so betrayed their own child, and herself.

In her book, *Incest: a Family Pattern*, Jean Renvoize, querying the notion that wives in incest families are normal and well adjusted, asks: 'Why should such a well-balanced woman pick such a man for her mate? Is anyone really quite as blind as that, even in the throes of love?'

Jan MacLeod, a community worker, in a paper for the women's support group in Glasgow, has aptly written:

A woman does not commit her life and security to a man she believes capable of molesting his own children.

Psychiatrists and experts in this field cannot find any 'identifying' features amongst abusers – so how are women supposed to identify an abuser before they marry him?

People will very readily talk about 'colluding mothers' but we should ask ourselves: if you were told, or began to suspect, that your brother or husband or friend was abusing his children, would you go straight to the police?

In (their) powerless position women are expected to be more aware, more resourceful and more courageous than the doctors, teachers, social workers, etc., who make up a society which through denial colludes with child abuse. Professional workers often condemn 'colluding mothers' in one breath, and in the next say 'I'm sure that there is incest in such and such a family, but I don't know what to do about it'.

None of these considerations seems to have dampened the enthusiasm of many advocates of family therapy who are determined that mothers must accept their dollop of responsibility for what took place. Sometimes it can be a hefty dollop, as in Hank Giaretto's much-vaunted and 'humanistic' treatment programme in California. He writes cheerfully:

While the mother's strong sense of guilt declines during the course of treatment, as does the father's, she, too, learns to accept her share of responsibility for the conditions leading to the molestation. By termination (of treatment) 50 per cent of the evaluator's sample admit that they were 'very much responsible' as opposed to none who admitted this at intake. This change of attitude comes from learning that incest is in large part due to a failing marriage, for which both spouses are responsible.

What very stubborn and recalcitrant women were coming through his door!

Several points emerge clearly from the analyses we have discussed.

The first is the rigidly traditional view of 'proper' relationships between husbands and wives, mothers and children. Dobash and Dobash remind us:

The psychoanalytic ideology concerning the normal, or healthy, relationship between males and females is extremely patriarchal ... the male, if he is to have a healthy, masculine identity, must be dominant and independent. The healthy female, on the other hand, is to take on such feminine characteristics as dependence, subordination to masculine authority, nurturance, service to others, and identification through them.

Early childhood learning is also seen as vital to healthy adult development and since mothers are supposed to be responsible for child care, they also play the crucial role in ensuring the child's well-being.

So, time and again, the woman is blamed for 'abdicating her role' as wife and mother. By the same process the husband is constantly excused responsibility. It cannot be his fault if she finds their sex life unpleasant or unsatisfying, if her home life is monotonous drudgery. She should put up with it, not leave him open to the temptations of incest by absenting herself because of a job or social interest. Even illness seems to be a luxury in which wives cannot afford to indulge. As Audrey Middleton writes: 'All mothers, then, according to the Justices, must be 'collusive'; which of us has never been tired, pregnant, depressed, sick, gone out to work, or out for an evening?'

Noreen Winchester's mother had 16 pregnancies, was constantly beaten by her husband yet still went out to work: he kept them chronically short of money, even for food. She is now in a mental institution. I was told by both lawyers and social workers that Mrs Winchester was a very bad mother while her husband was a good father, though perhaps 'too strict'.

We can also see that fathers are not expected to take their turn at giving their children the 'nurturing, affectionate relationship' they need. That is the mother's duty. They are not even expected to be able to restrain their aggressive, masculine drives, Tormes comments 'Considering the father as a possible source of control of incest seems ... like considering the fox ... as guard in the henhouse.'

The second point is the comical inconsistency of these writers. They put mothers in a classic 'catch-22'. On the one hand, they are blamed for showing signs of independence. On the other, they are said to be too dependent on their husbands, not to say 'infantile'. One might have thought, for instance, that taking a job would be a way of avoiding the financial reliance on husbands, which deters some wives from reporting incest. One can also speculate on what Mrs Winchester's rating as a 'dutiful mother' would have been had she not gone out to earn money for food but let her children starve.

The whole doublethink and prejudice which characterises professional attitudes to mothers was excellently captured by Dietz and Craft. They found that even though most of their social workers believed mothers were physically intimidated, 87 per cent also believed the mothers gave 'unconscious consent' to the incest, while 65 per cent believed mothers shared 'equal responsibility' with the fathers for incest. Yet at the same time, almost half considered the wives were 'submissive to their husband's authority.'

Probing the contradictions further, Dietz and Craft discovered that due to lack of training and a sense of inadequacy in the face of incest, social workers relied heavily on the professional literature to make sense of the problem. This literature told them that mothers consented and were equally, or fully, to blame.

It becomes clear that biased views of women continue to be passed on to workers through the professional literature, and that workers tend to cling to such biases even when presented with evidence to the contrary.

Blaming the mother was also a way of coping with their sense of failure at being unable to prevent repeated incestuous abuse.

The final point about these theories is their basic implication. This is that mothers would better protect their daughters, and be more willing to help them through therapy, if they behaved more like 'traditional' wives and mothers.

But the evidence points far more strongly to exactly the opposite conclusion.

It seems from many accounts, like those of Herman and Hirschman, that many incest victims' mothers suffer low self-esteem (67 per cent of Dietz and Craft's social workers noted this). They are often treated as 'doormats' by their husbands, believe what those husbands tell them about themselves, suffer physical and verbal abuse, and feel they have no choice but to accept their husband's authority. Few have experienced a fulfilling sexual relationship: few expect this is something women can find or demand. Florence Rush writes:

My mother's inability to protect me from sexual abuse (not in this case incestuous abuse) did not occur because she was worse than any other mother, but because, like all women, she was guilty and repulsed by her own sexuality and taught me to feel the same way.

In other words, by their very acceptance of subordination and inequality in marriage, of passive and guilty sexuality, these women are already 'traditional' wives and mothers.

In one of her sympathetic bouts, Forward writes:

> The typical mother ... finds herself in a position of having to take sides in a conflict between her husband and her daughter ... she may become paralysed by these alternatives and sink into severe depression.

The point about this conflict of loyalty is that only a 'traditional' mother would be defeated by it. As Dietz and Craft point out, overriding loyalty to one's husband is a classic traditional family value for women. This conflicts with an equally sacred traditional duty – to protect one's children. 'Submissive' wives are caught horribly between two socially prescribed 'supportive' roles: positive action requires an assertiveness she has learned not to practise, and which she is ill-equipped to adopt. 'To point an accusing finger at a woman caught in such a dilemma,' says Dietz and Craft, 'is inconsistent with social work values of respect for the individual and nondiscriminatory treatment.'

More proof of traditionalism comes through in mothers' reactions to daughters' accusations. Why do some say, 'You just have to put up with it', or 'You must have asked for it'? Why do some make excuses like, 'He just needs a lot of sex', or call their daughters whores and sluts? And why can it seem so terrifying to challenge the husband that disbelieving the daughter is an easier choice?

What comes through vividly from these mothers is that they share the same traditional assumptions as their husbands, their daughters, and the 'experts'. The girls must have encouraged it, done something shameful and dirty. If the husbands succumbed, well men are like that, they need a lot of sex and can't resist temptation. You are not supposed to challenge your husband and if you do, you pay a heavy price. The prospect of surviving without him, or having him removed from the home, is frightening because independence is not part of your experience.

It even seems impossible to discuss what's happening with your daughter, because sex is so hard to talk about, and it makes you confront your own vulnerability, your own unsatisfactory or humiliating experience. It is easier to accept the situation fatalistically, however painful this is, because you expect and already know that women will be exploited by men.

A number of writers, like Forward, have condemned mothers' refusal to join in the therapeutic process and allow their daughters to work through feelings of rage and betrayal. Their central theme is that mothers will not take responsibility for their part in the incestuous abuse. Treatment programmes as we have seen are also geared to making both parents accept their role in the incest, and help the victim see she is not to blame.

One cannot help but wonder if the opposite approach might be more successful in encouraging mothers to enter therapy and thus help 'free' their daughters: if a consciousness-raising programme was run which repaired mothers' self-esteem, instead of demanding that they accept a still greater burden of guilt. It is on this basis that feminist organisations are now increasingly running groups for mothers of survivors.

This would involve the revolutionary step of suggesting to mothers that they were not to blame for being ill, depressed or pregnant, for finding sex unfulfilling, for going to work or splashing out on bingo once a week. But it would mean getting them to question the consequences of their traditional family values, and how these prevented the mother from reporting or stopping the abuse. This could also help daughters greatly, by giving them insight into their mothers' dilemmas and conflicts, and helping them to understand why the immensely painful betrayal happened as it did.

One can only speculate how differently mothers might have behaved when daughters first sought their help, if they believed women deserved the same respect, independence and sexual fulfilment as men. If they rejected the idea that women should ever be used as sexual objects, if they valued themselves and their daughters as much as their husbands, they might find it considerably easier to overcome the conflicts of loyalty and 'duty' that currently overwhelm so many mothers. But current professional theory and practice positively discourages 'collusive wives' from even starting to move towards such dangerous and unwifely notions.

THE MEN

Rationalisation theories for the male offender

It will be obvious by now that the male offender has not been the centre of attention for professionals who have tried to explain why incest happens. When they do consider him, they usually see his actions as the result of some abnormality, or distinctiveness from the rest of the community. This view is probably shared by the public at large.

On the whole, these offenders are treated either dismissively or sympathetically by professionals. One gets a very widespread impression from reading, but more especially from discussion, that most would agree with Forward's view 'Most incest aggressors are not really criminals, and do not need to be locked up.' Unlike many other crimes, incest seems to inspire strong professional concern about how the offender can be helped, and how he can be kept close to his family.

He may be seen as an individual deviant; as a member of a deviant subculture; as part of a historic cycle of family abuse; or as part of an abnormal, dysfunctional family. None of these theories relates his behaviour to the whole system of social values about sexuality and the family, in which he exists.

Faced with more evidence about the diverse social backgrounds of incest offenders, a growing minority of 'experts' question deviance theories, and state that these men may be 'Mr Average'. But they still do not criticise average social values for contributing to violation of the taboo. Instead, they tend to excuse the man's behaviour, either by referring to what they see as natural male instincts, or by blaming other family members for some fault or another.

The smallest group of writers link fathers' behaviour directly to traditional patriarchal values about the family, values which society is reluctant to challenge.

Myth: the man is a deviant

> 'I mean, there's got to be something wrong or ill about a father who does that sort of thing to his daughter.'

Mental illness and alcoholism have been the leading types of individual abnormalities described by researchers. For instance Phillip found 50 per cent of his sample were alcoholics 'and a great number were imbeciles'. Some writers have even found 'atrophy of the frontal lobes'.

Deviant sexual traits are also frequently reported. The problem about these findings is that they are often contradictory. Some men are found to be undersexed, others oversexed. Some experts believe the men are unconscious homosexuals, others that they are uninhibited heterosexuals. A few, like Weinberg, hedge their bets by claiming their subjects fall into several categories, in his case, the indiscriminately promiscuous, the psychosexually immature with paedophiliac cravings, etc. There are the usual Freudian weaves: Cormier and Kubo describe the father's attempt to see his daughter the wife of his youth, in whom he unconsciously saw a substitute of his first love (yes, you've guessed it), his mother.

Several writers note how some offenders are prone to violence, like to exert power over their families or tyrannise them, and stop them making social contacts outside the home. But this is seen as an individual deviation from normal husbands' behaviour. Forward describes offenders like this, but does not believe they form the majority of incestuous fathers. Likewise the Kempes state:

We do find men with psychopathic personalities and indiscriminate sexuality, who view children as objects. But most fathers ... are introverted personalities who tend to be socially isolated and family-oriented. *(sic)*

Other writers stress subcultural, rather than family, deviance. The men's actions are explained by a cluster of characteristics believed to be common among lower working class people. Lukianowicz pointed out that none of her sample was psychotic or frankly neurotic. But their habitual unemployment and other feckless tendencies suggested inadequate and anti-social personalities. She felt incest might be an accepted form of behaviour among aggressive, oversexed males in certain subcultures. She also described the typical 'lower class' profile of the incest offender. Researchers had noted factors like poverty, poor education, overcrowding etc. These subcultures, of course, also drink rather heavily (unlike doctors or lawyers). The idea that drink 'causes' incest seems to be a popular public belief, and finds echoes in the literature. Drink, of course, is also supposed to 'cause' wife beating, and numerous other crimes.

We need hardly repeat the problems about these two theories, as we have already discussed class biased sampling, especially of convicted offenders. Again, no one would deny that some incest offenders, just like other criminals, will be abnormal or have severe social problems. Whether the bulk of incest can be explained in this way is quite another question.

Myth: the man is a product of his family history

On this theory, men abuse their children because they themselves were abused as children. In turn, their own offspring are likely to become abusers. The sins of the father are visited on the children, and so on through the generations. Often, it is claimed that their wives were also victims of molestation, and have consciously or subconsciously picked an abusive husband.

Thus Renvoize states 'What has become clear is that, just as with physical abuse, history endlessly repeats itself … an abused childhood leads to an abusive parenthood.' She points out, for instance, that in his study of juvenile offenders Wenet found 54 per cent of those referred for sexual molestation had themselves been victims of sexual or physical abuse.

This theory will be familiar to students of the 'cycle of poverty' or the 'cycle of violence'. It is often said that husbands batter wives because they themselves were beaten in their youth. The battering bug, like the incest bug, is carried around in the genes like a permanent dose of measles.

No one would deny that some violent or abusive men were ill treated as children, and find it especially difficult as a result to relate in loving or secure ways to others. But there are several serious problems about this as a general explanation of incest, or of any form of domestic violence.

First, bets are hedged by woolly definitions of the damage fathers faced: this is often said to include sexual, physical or emotional abuse. A great percentage of the British population could come into this category!

Secondly, when it is confined to sexual assault, this implies that the sexual abuse of males is a huge, unrevealed social problem. If hundreds of thousands of incestuous fathers, brothers and uncles were themselves victims, who assaulted them? Proponents of this theory must come up with the proof and the statistics.

Thirdly, we again face the difficulty that 'problem families' with a long history of conflict and instability have been over-represented in the samples from which therapists, criminologists and researchers draw their conclusions. But survivors' accounts give a far more diverse picture of the family history of their abusers.

Fourthly, the theorists use no control group against which to compare their sample. Yet that group may be far bigger and more representative than this sample. Numerous British or American fathers had unhappy or violent childhoods, but the majority do not go on to commit incest with their children. Likewise, many men who watched their fathers beat their mothers do not batter their own wives. Why is this? Cycle of violence theorists have no satisfactory answer. But clearly human reaction to violent example or suffering varies greatly, and copycat explanations fail to fit thousands, or millions, of people.

The theory's most serious fault is that it is ahistorical, unconnected with the wider society and its values. It hangs meaninglessly in the air, or goes round in circles. Where did all this abuse spring from? The only answer is: from the parents, and the great grandparents, and ultimately, one supposes, from some caveman and his colluding wife.

But why did the men behave like that, what made them think it was acceptable and that they could get away with it? Why did the wives and children put up with it? Why did no one from the rest of society intervene to stop it?

The message behind this theory is a familiar one. The cycle of abuse affects a minority of men and their families, who can be numbered and contained and treated, and put on a happier road. They have nothing in common with your family or mine. Instead, they have got society's values wrong. Those values have done nothing to encourage their behaviour.

Insofar as abuse does repeat itself through generations, there is a more convincing explanation than incest bugs or copycat behaviour. It is that people learn a set of values from a parent or the wider society which rationalises their abusive behaviour, their suffering, or their failure to intervene. We shall consider this again in discussion of patriarchal theories of incest.

Myth: A normal man has to have sex

'The poor fellow must have been driven to it.'

As we have already seen, more and more researchers have discovered that incestuous fathers may come from every social background and type of family. As early as 1937 Ebner had warned: 'It is not the mentally sick type, nor the hypersexual or sexually abnormal man, nor the man with the most inferior character, who is dominant among those committing incest.'

The much-quoted Maisch had found his 1,500 cases 'a completely heterogeneous picture'. Recently Forward has written from her own experience: 'He is rarely a freak, a dangerous criminal or a psychotic ... often an otherwise law-abiding, hardworking guy next door who ... has lost the ability to control his impulses.'

She found the average offender to be fairly intelligent, and quite a few were regular churchgoers.

Most explanations of incest among 'normal' men invoke mother blame. As already noted, most known incest offenders seem to fall within the 28–45 age group. So there has been a widespread assumption that they are reacting to natural problems, needs and temptations. Henderson notes: 'These are the years when marriage becomes increasingly frustrating, when death, separation and divorce occasionally provide a real basis for separation anxiety.'

The range and nature of the wife's failings have already been described. Temptations offered by growing daughters are also much discussed, even though the idea that puberty brings on initiation of incest is not supported by the evidence.

The assumption that there is something inevitable and natural in these temptations comes through in the comments of researchers like Hall-Williams. In his study of convicted men he noted the importance of things like a wife's absence from home. Instead of questioning the husband's assumptions, he suggested that social services departments might do more to prevent such situations becoming occasions for incestuous behaviour. He did not spell out if this meant removing the girl from home, installing a chaperone, or what!

We can note the apparent assumption that if the male's 'natural' needs are not met, it is not surprising if he turns to his daughter for them. Yet most men do not do this so what is normal about it? There are other problems about these theories, for example, some research has challenged the ready assumption that the men are enduring celibacy. For instance Lukianowicz pointed out that in her sample, 'Almost all these men had intercourse with their wives too, and two had mistresses'. Numerous accounts from incest survivors also challenge the view that the men were starved of other adult sexual relationships.

Again, the inadequacy of blaming other family members or 'a cruel society' for the man's actions is sometimes suggested by the very writers who want us to believe this.

For instance, Forward writes of grandfather–granddaughter incest:

It is our neglectful treatment of the aged that precipitates the majority of such cases and typically the older incestuous grandfather is a victim of society's assumption that ageing and deterioration are one.

So, it is said, they try and prove their manhood and beat their lone-liness by sexual relations with an uncritical child.

But her kindly explanation and pathetic picture hardly seems to fit the grandfather she actually describes in detail. This involved an unusual case of 'multiple personality', where a grown woman would adopt the facial expressions and voice of her grandfather, but could not recall this later.

Her face contorted with hate, she hissed things like 'You goddam son of a bitch whore, I'm gonna get you, you shithole'. It emerged that he had penetrated her with objects when she was a young child, and jumped at her from hiding places around the house, putting her in a state of terror. This man did not seem to have a very high respect or liking for the female sex: that point, or problem, is not discussed by Forward.

Myth: incest is a sign of a dysfunctional family

> 'It's a symptom of a sick, dysfunctional family with a dis-ordered role allocation.'

To other experts, the man isn't really looking for sex at all. No, he is looking for love in the wrong way. This theory has been so import-ant in family therapy that we will subsume it here under the family heading. This is not so incongruous as it looks, since a major tech-nique in classifying male offenders has been to invoke the whole family constellations as another important way of reducing re-sponsibility in these offenders.

Rosenfield writes 'From our clinical observations, it seems that incestuous relationships are often a distorted search for caring and warmth.' Forward feels a man's incestuous abuse is 'usually an attempt to find the tenderness and understanding that should issue from his relationship with his wife, but usually does not'.

Again, Hank Giaretto writes:

> 'the sexually abusive father does not use his child primarily for sexual gratification, but principally as a means of reconfirm-ing and discharging his low self-worth ... the hateful reactions of the counsellors towards abusive parents (sic) must be replaced with productive interventions, based on understand-ing of the complex psychological dynamics that led to the abus-ive acts'.

These theories are often put forward by abusers themselves,

especially if they have learned their scripts from therapists in 'humanistic' treatment programmes. Male offenders told Rich Snowdon, in his powerful and painfully honest paper *Excuses, excuses, excuses*, how they were giving their daughters gentle nurturance, or else they were seeking solace: 'My boss was critical of me all the time. My son was picked up by the police ... my wife couldn't stand to be around me any more. I was trying to take care of everything by myself. No one was looking after me. That's where my daughter came in.'

One advantage of this theory is that you do not have to be lower working class to distort your search for caring and warmth. Chaotic, disorganised lower class families will certainly be in the forefront: but any one can have a lapse, especially when weighed down by job and family stress. To cure the disease you cannot treat the offender in isolation, for the problem has deeper causes.

Besides role allocations throughout the family have become disordered and need sorting out. Where parents turn to children to fulfil their needs, role reversals are common, with daughters taking on the mothers' functions or young children meeting their grandfathers' sexual needs. Roles will be askew and intergenerational boundaries blurred: the therapist's task is to re-educate people into appropriate roles, feelings and nurturance and help them participate in the wider society's system of values. But this will be tough because once the dysfunctional family system gets going, it takes on a life of its own. This explains why incestuous abuse continues for so long, and why other family members may turn on the daughter for exposing it. The theorists say the system is tenacious because a precarious family stability is being maintained at the child's expense. The family's idiosyncratic solution to problems helps it to avoid painful realities. Members share meanings and beliefs which 'maintain the pathological surface action which contains the incestuous behaviour, and perpetuates it over long periods'.

We have entered the realms of systems theory. A dense jungle of jargon threatens to overwhelm. There is homeostasis and feed back circularity, there is over-involvement and disequilibrium, there is paradox and incongruity, and there are diagrams with arrows. Scribbled beside the arrows are abbreviations for each family member: Fa-Do-Mo, which sound like the latest Italian Soap Opera. Lay people have no chance of sharing this knowledge: only an expert can sort the problem out.

Most important, there are rigid boundaries against the outside world. Knowledge and disagreements are kept inside the family, it is said, because otherwise it would disintegrate. This helps to explain why many incestuous families seem to be 'endogamic', isolated from others and self sufficient. Indeed the endogamic family has become a category in itself, as a prime candidate for incest. This would seem to confuse cause and effect.

But 'now is the time for the social worker, therapist or judge to intervene and assume the role of family disequalizer or 'psycho-shaker', according to Beezley Mrazek and Bentovim. The intervention they urge is admirably jargon-free, e.g. 'Dad's a cuddler, is he? Does he ever give Mom a cuddle, too?' This, they say, puts the focus back on the 'spouse subsystem'.

A full critique of systems theory cannot be attempted here. It is important only to stress its major flaw. This is not the jargon, but what the gobbledygook is actually saying. Family members are treated as equals: no source is given for the decisions that are arrived at. They coalesce out of the air. Who is isolating the family from contact or preventing a girl mixing with boyfriends? Who takes the decisions and enforces them? Who persuades a six year old girl into oral sex with her grandfather? The system?

The theory takes little or no account of power structures within families, reinforced or tacitly supported by the wider society. Power in most families is unequal: where a father is authoritarian or physically abusing his wife and children, it may be grossly so. Unless your theory can accommodate such a basic and vital consideration, it is fluttering about in cloud cuckoo land. Sandra Butler has sent a short reminder through the mist to its proponents: 'Families don't assault children sexually. Men do'. Survivors and their mothers will also wish to assert that shared meanings were not a feature of their experience. Their accounts of what it meant and felt like, of how it started and why it continued, have been very different from those of abusers and professionals – as this book has shown. Those who believed meanings were shared were either not listening to the unauthorised versions or chose to dismiss them.

The abuse of male power

Finally we turn to theories which place the responsibility for incestuous abuse on the male offender, whose actions are encouraged or excused by values which are held widely throughout society.

Feminist explanations of paternal incest see social beliefs about 'normal' male sexuality and 'normal' family roles as positive contributors to incest. These assumptions, they feel, must be challenged head-on, not excused as natural or immutable.

Forward, who seems to work her way through every theory under the sun, says at one point:

> Too often a father views his daughter as his sexual property, to exploit as he sees fit ... the concept of daughter as sexual chattel is probably responsible for weakening the taboo against father–daughter incest.

This theory is then dropped and sinks without trace in a sea of words about nurturance, etc.

Writers like Herman and Hirschman have pursued it, however. They believe seduction of daughters is inherent in a father-dominated family system, where the man expects to have his will obeyed as head of household, and expects his family to provide him with domestic and sexual services. When wives are no longer able to provide them he will not expect to perform them himself but will look elsewhere and some will turn to the eldest daughter, the 'next in line'. This theory sees the father, not the mother, as dominant in pushing daughters into the maternal role. His actions are the result of his rigid social beliefs about family roles and duties.

The authors suggest 'We may expect violations of the taboo to occur most frequently in families characterised by extreme paternal dominance.' This would explain why researchers so often find incest offenders to be 'family tyrants' as, indeed, most of the social workers in Dietz and Craft's study did.

Support for this analysis would seem to come from a study of convicted offenders (incestuous men, wifebeaters and family non-supporters) by Scheurell and Rinder. They note that the first group have the highest role segregation within the family, with the greatest number of tasks performed by female children. They consider that incest offenders have a need to manipulate their kin grouping by restructuring roles within the family, so as to reduce their own tasks as far as possible.

But this turns upside-down conventional theory about disorganised families, with their disordered role allocations. The assumption was that these families had moved away from normal family values, and had made chaos out of order. On the contrary, Scheurell and Rinder's offenders could be seen as trying to re-impose order out of chaos. They were trying to restore what they believed to be the normal, traditional pattern of things in a patriarchal family where they were served, and took on as a few family responsibilities as possible within the home.

Susan Brownmiller also argues that wider social assumptions about patriarchy positively discourage outside intervention in crimes like incest. 'The taboo against father-rape is superseded by a stronger, possibly older taboo – that there shall be no outside interference in the absolute dictatorshop of father-rule.'

Today's gentler, liberal phrase tends to be: 'keeping the family together as far as possible'. But the consequences for wife and children may not be very different than they would have been if Brownmiller's harsh reasoning still pervaded social agencies.

Florence Rush makes a still harsher judgment on the social function of paternal incest:

> The sexual abuse of children is an early manifestation of male power and oppression of the female ... (it is) an unspoken but prominent factor in socialising and preparing the female to accept a subordinate role ... prepares her to submit later to the sexual abuse heaped on her by her boyfriend, lover and husband.

Some people may argue that many incest offenders do not invoke patriarchal beliefs to explain their actions. But we should bear in mind that beliefs do not have to be highly worked-out and articulated before they influence behaviour. The 'family tyrant' type of offender, who is usually violent to his wife and children, may indeed have clear views on his rights as head of household even if he is reticent about actually telling experts, courts or neighbours that he believes he has a right to sex with his daughter. (For though many people still believe 'Blokes have a right to slap their wives, don't they?' and wifebeaters will often appeal to others in this way, most members of the public would be horrified or repulsed by the claim that men had a right to sex with their daughters.)

With other husbands, however, patriarchal theories are more likely to have a diffuse, negative effect than a clearcut, positive one. In other words, instead of actively propelling the men into incest, they reduce the emotional and other barriers to overcoming the taboo—to taking risks that may lead to disgrace or imprisonment. Just as important, they are likely to reduce feelings of guilt about succumbing to temptation.

Beliefs that can influence in these ways include:

Men (like me) naturally need a lot of sex, I can't be expected to wait while my wife is in hospital;

Everyone knows men lose control and do daft things when they're drunk, I wouldn't do it normally;

I mean, you don't expect blokes to do the ironing and cooking and cleaning if the wife's out at work, your daughter should do it shouldn't she?;

Daughters ought to do what they're told by their fathers, you expect that;

Blokes get led on by women, it's not fair, it happens all the time;

They pretend they don't like it, they act virtuous, but they love it really;

Flaunting herself at me all the time like that, she's asking for it, besides she must be a bad girl if she goes on doing it;

At least she's under my control, not messing about all hours of the night with boys and getting into trouble like some of them, I'm not having that.

This often contradictory mish-mash of possessiveness, self-justification, assumptions about rights to control, beliefs that women lead men on and forfeit respect when they submit; all this still runs through the thinking of many men in their general relationships with women, from adolescence onwards. When residual, patriarchal beliefs about rights of fathers provide further excuses for initiating sexually gratifying relationships within the family, it is not hard to see how many 'Mr Averages' can manage to overcome all the social and emotional barriers to committing incest with their daughters. This explanation of incest as the simple abuse of power and position, fuelled by belittling views of women, has been rejected by many theorists and therapists. It is too simplistic, they say; it does not fit most of the cases they see; it does not square with the anxious offenders who seem so meek and mild to the outside world, and to them.

Survivors have a simpler and harsher memory of the reality. Emily Driver of the Incest Survivors Campaign in London has told professional audiences:

Why are grown people so frightened of the facts? Because I had to face them as a child, I had no horror of the truth as such. What I feared was my abuser. For me incest was the deepest form of dishonesty. Therefore I feared my abuser and respected the truth. On turning to the outside world for an explanation of my experience, what do I find? That professionals respect my abuser, and fear the truth.

The truth is simple. That a man or boy has put his whim for mere sexual gratification before the survival needs of a child.

We want you to see the Emperor without his clothes, as we have seen him. The incest abuser is a bully. A bully is a man intent on power. If you have more than him, if you are above him, he will suck up to you; if you are below him, he will stamp on your face.

It is said that these are the views of damaged, embittered women, or of man-haters, or both. Let us turn then to the experience of Rich Snowdon, who led counselling groups for male offenders in San Francisco. He expected to find psychopaths and monsters; he found ordinary men, who reminded him of himself, whose explanations and excuses were all too profoundly familiar.

I was less and less able to deny how much we had in common. We grew up learning the same things about how to be men ... we were taught that privilege is our birthright and aggression is our nature, so we learned to take, not to give. We expected to marry a woman who would provide for us like a mother, but obey us like a daughter. And we learned that women and children belong to men, that there is nothing to keep us from using their labour for our benefit and their bodies for our pleasure and anger.

When he started thinking about incest abusers, he had to start thinking of the ordinary men of America.

Therapists generally report that incest offenders are non-threatening men, that they are charmers and wimps ... taken by surprise one night in the group, I found that just a little pushing will bring out what's really below the surface. I started a discussion about enforcing Court orders and there was suddenly a tightening of muscles, a clenching of teeth, and a pounding of fists ... I sat there amid the rising anger, a grown man, and was afraid.

I could only think about a child facing one of these men alone. The fear she must feel. The bottomless anger she must know is there ... even when he is opening his needs to her like a beggar, she must know that her father is still her master and she must either obey or risk his rage ... incest offenders are men who simply have the power to take what they want, and who take it.

Yet from start to finish, he found, most offenders denied what they had done, and claimed they were the true victims. The first self-deception story was 'Lolita'. Their daughters were demon nymphettes: 'these men are as fast as TV scriptwriters and as facile as professional pornographers, the way they turn out line after line about the dangerous desires of little girls and how they are always getting men into trouble.'

The second deception was the 'wicked witch', to whom each of them seemed to be married. A well-meaning, natural father was browbeaten by an insistent, controlling wife into doing something terrible to his children.

It's a contagious excuse. Once one man in a group picks up on it, there's an epidemic. Yet one night when I reminded Quentin that he couldn't miss even one session ... he shouted back 'Don't tell me what to do. Nobody is going to make me do anything I don't wanna.' He couldn't have made it clearer. No woman and no child makes a man commit an assault.

The third deception is Santa Claus as the generous father, who was just giving his daughter nurturance or a gentle sex education, who was a sincere and misguided parent. A few set aside the Santa disguise and reveal the truth with a terrible but honest arrogance: 'She told me, no I don't want to. But I just said, shut up, you have to.' These fathers acknowledge that they could do what they did only because they could make their children obey and could command silence ... yet it is this very power that most men deny when they are caught and convicted.

Suddenly, Snowdon says, they are incapable of controlling their own actions. They couldn't help themselves and were helpless prey in the face of Lolita. They believe they are heroes if they refuse to succumb, and ordinary guys if they give in.

As long as these men deny their own power and the power of men as a group, they also deny the responsibility men share, and so nothing changes. They deny that they can respond to stress with solutions instead of assault ... they deny that they can change themselves: 'My conditioning made me do it.' Or, 'I'm sick ... I'm evil' ...

Lamont explained, as we were sitting by his window looking out through the bars: 'We all knew what we were doing was wrong, but we each had stories we told ourselves, so we could keep on doing it.' Lolita, the wicked witch and Santa Claus are those stories. They are not tales men read to their daughters and sons at bedtime to help them fall peacefully asleep, but stories they make their children live. Stories of endless terror.

Most therapists have helped abusers maintain their self-deceptive stories. Often enough, they have handed them the scripts. The experience of one of Snowden's clients suggests a more effective method of change.

'Carlos' had watched a TV programme where an incest survivor had told the story of her life.

He had broken down and cried his way through the programme, listening for the first time with his heart, not with his defenses, and at last had begun to understand his daughter's terror. It was with the truth from the point of view of the child and the woman that therapy started.

Snowdon concludes:

When we were boys, we didn't have the power to stop lies and violence, but now that we are men, we do. We have the power to stand with boys who are growing up and help them defend their caring. We have the power to stop being 'ordinary guys' and become something much better. Men with whom children and women can be safe.

Dealing with male offenders: imprisonment, treatment, change

Professional theories about why men commit incest have strongly affected attitudes about how male offenders should be dealt with.

There is a widespread view that imprisonment is not appropriate for such men. Forward, for instance, notes:

I spoke with more than three dozen judges, commissioners, lawyers, police officers, social workers ... and psychologists, and their responses were almost identical: unless they (offenders) demonstrate some abnormal tendency towards violence, they should generally be sentenced to treatment rather than prison.

Likewise, though 78 per cent of Dietz and Craft's social workers suspected their offenders physically abused their wives, and 76 per cent suspected physical child abuse, most believed the father should not be incarcerated. A majority said he should be removed from the home, without spelling out what this meant. Opposition to imprisonment is also widespread among professionals in Britain.

There are three major reasons behind this view. The first is that the man does not deserve to be punished: imprisonment is inappropriate and ineffective. The second is that prison breaks up the family and that it is desirable, for ideological reasons, to keep families together or to repair broken ones. The third reason is more practical. Whether breakup is morally desirable or not, it puts social and economic stresses on family members who lose their breadwinner, and places a huge burden of guilt on the child. Victims, it is said, might be much more willing to speak out if they knew their father, grandfather or brother would not go to jail.

I would like to make some considerations here about these three points.

Anyone who advocates treatment on the grounds that it is appropriate for the male offender must be quite clear about the implications of what they are saying. It means the men are sick, deviant, abnormal or inadequate. Alternatively, it means that they bear less responsibility for their actions than other types of offender whose disposal is via the penal system. In particular, family treatment programmes imply that responsibility must be shared, especially by the wife.

Many of the arguments in this book have directly challenged such assumptions, and the forms of treatment which result. Further repetition would labour the point. Professionals (especially pro-feminists) and others who support the criticisms but still believe treatment is a good idea must ask if they have sorted out their ideas fully, and if they have looked critically enough at treatment programmes lauded as examples to follow. We are not just talking about the flaws in family pathology theories, or mother-blame. We are also talking about assumptions that may be as irresponsible and naive as they are humane and charitable. Some American programmes held up as examples only offer treatment alternatives to nonviolent first offenders. What is a nonviolent incest offender? Where do you draw the exact line between coercion by adult authority and veiled threat, and coercion by overt force? How often are incest offenders exposed after their first offence? Whose word do you take on it? Most have been offending for years. This type of nonsense should be described for what it is.

The idea that families should be kept together because this is right also underpins many family treatment programmes. Hank Giaretto lists the first goal of the Child Sexual Abuse Treatment Programme, San Jose, as rehabilitation of the family and the marriage. The idea that families should be helped to stay together has also been tenacious in social work practice in general.

However laudable their aims, practitioners must realise that this is not a neutral position. It is what most male offenders want: it is not necessarily what other family members either want or need. They may pay a heavy price for reunification. An alternative view is that the male offender has forfeited his right to any say in the matter, since he has already betrayed his family's trust and destroyed the family unit.

The Kempes have written: 'Reuniting families should not be the overriding goal. Rather, the best interests of the child should be served...' Children and their mothers surely have the right to expect that professionals will take the time and trouble to assess, in the absence of pressure from the offender, what they really want to happen in the future, and with whom they wish to live. Lucy Berliner of the Harborview project in Seattle has said:

People do not encourage kids to say, hey, I don't ever want to see you (Dad) again. Whenever did you see any support for a kid saying that? Here we don't tell kids what to feel... whatever they feel, we say to them, that's normal, if that is what you feel, that's fine.

Those who genuinely believe every effort should be made to keep incestuous families together should also ask why it is only in family crimes, and only in certain family crimes, that calls go out for victim and offender to be kept together.

No one would suggest that muggers, burglars or rapists should live with their victims in the same house for the next five or ten years. The very idea would provoke laughter or outrage. Still fewer people would suggests that parents proved or suspected of battering their children should be left to continue. Indeed social work agencies, scapegoated by the media, have grown cautious to the point of paranoia about preventing this family crime, and removing children at risk from the home. Broken limbs are widely equated with violence and child abuse: incest, despite the physical and mental harm it causes, does not appear to be in the same way.

The experience of battered wives also suggests that family violence is especially likely to be repetitive. Here we are not just talking about repeats of the original crime, but pressure and continual harassment and visits while a man is out on bail, at a probation hostel, or under an exclusion order. This is a major problem about violence against the person in the home. The family's need for continued physical protection and separation is greater, not less, than it is in other types of crime.

We must also ask why professional agencies and others are so selective in their concern about the effects of breaking up the family.

Many things break up families: for instance Government policy can increase homelessness or family stress.

Unemployment is one major source of this. Imprisonment always separates families, and often breaks them up for good. Every day in our courts, married men and women with children are sent to prison, many for trivial offences. With little protest, our legal and social work agencies tolerate and work for a system in which our penal institutions are heavily over-represented with unskilled working class people, disadvantaged racial groups, and minor property offenders.

Only a minority of professionals have lobbied against the prison visiting system and its effects on the family unit. Only a minority have suggested that the con-man or housebreaker should not be removed from his family, or protested about women who defraud social security of £10 being removed from their children and home.

Property offenders threaten sections of the wider community: incest aggressors, within their own four walls, do not.

It seems generally acceptable to imprison and remove from their families people who are not a danger to their families. It is not, apparently, acceptable to remove people who really are a danger to their families, because this might break up the home. This seems slightly ironic. We would also want to ask how, given the evidence presented here and elsewhere, people would compare the damage done by an incest offender and a social security defrauder.

All these considerations are relevant to the practical set of objections to imprisonment discussed earlier. Other issues also need to be raised.

Prison may be useless in many ways. It may suck in the undeserving, and fail to rehabilitate offenders. But it does have one useful function: it is the only method our society has devised of expressing its most serious condemnation of certain acts, by proclaiming: 'We cannot tolerate these values or actions'.

Many supporters of penal reform, including myself, wish our places of ultimate sanction were different, and more constructive. But so long as prisons fill this role, there are dangers in pleading that certain offences be decriminalised. For you cannot remove or reduce responsibility from a crime without also making a statement about its gravity in the eyes of society.

In recent years, feminists in particular have protested at the light sentences many men receive on conviction for violent assaults against women. Most of the protest is not about vengeance, but rather people seek stronger sentences for what these represent as a statement. 'This is a serious crime; society must regard it as such, not turn a blind eye or condone with a wink the way some men treat women and children'.

Incest has strong links with other sex crimes, like rape, and other family crimes, like wife-beating. It is difficult to see how some pro-feminists can demand increased penalties for one set of crimes, reduced penalties for another. They should also ask themselves how happy they would feel if a new treatment programme was set up for rapists, or if wife-beaters and their families entered therapy as a means of keeping the family unit together.

As society begins to take incest seriously and the damage it does, it will move up the scale of relative seriousness as a crime. In these circumstances, pleas for leniency would only make sense if they were also applied to crimes considered equally serious.

For survivors, the problems of reporting and testifying are real. But should they be met by means which also weaken the statement we make about the crime, especially if this leads to treatment that is inappropriate for offender, mother and victim?

The logic of this discussion is that we can only talk about softer treatment for incest offenders in the context of reformed sentencing for all offenders. Within the present system, there is no reason why incest abusers should be treated more leniently than others, and many reasons, in terms of criteria like danger, damage and deterrence for the sake of prevention, why they should be regarded as serious criminals relative to other offenders.

Liberals should not, I believe, be intimidated from saying that most incest offenders should have to serve a jail term because of the statement by society which this represents. But this in itself will not be enough. Because of what we know of the lifelong damage incestuous abuse causes, two goals are especially important. One is to try to change the offenders' future behaviour, and the other is to safeguard potential victims against repetition of assaults. Our prisons, as they are, can be relied on to do neither.

Whether programmes for change take place within prison or after release, they should be compulsory. Nearly all treatment programmes nowadays, either good, bad or indifferent accept that incest offenders are especially reluctant to maintain voluntary treatment, and need some kind of legal sanction attached to any programme.

What type of programme offers most hope of changing the behaviour of at least some incest offenders? The experience of Rich Snowdon and others suggests that what will not change it is fortification of the men's own excuses for their actions. In group discussion they must not be allowed to support each other's justifications or find such support from the therapist. Self-help has to be interventionist where offenders are concerned.

The offenders must be forced to challenge their assumptions about family roles, sexuality, masculinity, and general relationships between men and women. They must also be made to confront survivors' experience, and what it meant to them, as Snowdon has suggested. Tapes and videos may be effective enough: no survivor should be asked to take part personally unless she can cope fully with the experience and has given truly free consent. She should never be pressured into such an exercise by being told it will secure a relative's early release.

Sympathetic men often ask what role they can play in combating sexual abuse, especially those who are aware that male participation in female therapy can pose serious problems for those they are trying to help. One answer is: change the behaviour of other men, by challenging it and saying that you find it unacceptable. Male workers could have a vital role to play in taking offenders' groups and working out programmes. Organisations like Sheffield Men Against Sexual Harassment have already put together excellent ideas for combating violence against women and working with male groups, and deserve more consultation on the innovations they have to offer others.

Taking protective action against future abuse means taking seriously the findings of intervention projects like Harborview that sexual abusers are especially vulnerable to re-offence, whatever remorse they express or feel. That in turn means taking seriously the need to ensure that offenders and their families are separated for as long as the families wish it, which means effective use of measures like exclusion orders and also implies that regulations about checking and recording past sex offences will need to be tightened. This is especially true where offenders move to other parts of the country and where they apply to work in any way with children.

We still have to remember that measures to deal with identified offenders can hardly scratch the problem of incest, since only a tiny minority will be reported or convicted. Few professionals have yet addressed themselves to the whole question of prevention.

Many people now acknowledge that deep-rooted social attitudes encourage crimes like wife-beating and rape: that until these attitudes are changed, no amount of work with convicted offenders will seriously reduce these crimes. Making the same mental connections about incest could be the biggest step towards long term prevention.

Among the priorities for professional and voluntary workers would be:

> Actively challenging, in their own workplaces, traditional values about sexuality and family roles, and pointing out how these still infuse professional practice; forcing their agencies or professions to confront their reluctance to intervene in family violence.

> Taking part in, and encouraging, publicity and campaign work among women and children. Teachers, medical workers and those who work in the media are particularly important to this work.

> Encouraging conditions where men would be deterred from committing incest in the first place, through fear of instant exposure. This means creating an atmosphere where survivors and their mothers feel free to seek professional help quickly without fear, embarrassment or shame.

Which way forward?

Many people will react to books like this by protesting: 'Reams of pages of theorising are all very well, but they seem like a luxury: what do we actually do about the problem now? How can we find all these unidentified victims, or set up a treatment centre next month?'

This reaction is understandable, but has many pitfalls and dangers because it starts at the wrong end. Theory comes before practice, not the other way round.

It is easy to draw up guidance notes advising agencies how to locate cases of incestuous abuse. But there is no point in finding these people if agencies don't know what to do with them. Without a clear policy programme, large-scale investigation could be irresponsible in its effects. Agencies often feel helpless enough in dealing with the cases they do know about. If social workers, psychiatrists, teachers or other groups worked hard to identify many more abused women and children, what kind of help could they offer people whose hopes had been raised?

Survivors have a right to know, before they share their experience with others, what help they can expect and what kind of treatment they will be asked to take part in. On the one hand, they need more than a mere sympathetic ear and the promise of confidentiality. As one social worker put it at an Edinburgh seminar on incest: 'It's not confidentiality they're seeking, it's someone to break it – someone who can safely bring what's happened into the open.'

On the other hand, if a comprehensive treatment programme is on offer, and that seems essential if agencies are not to lose trust and effectiveness by contradicting each other's policies, those who are abused will want to know what ideas underpin the programme. For instance if mothers are expected to shoulder a large part of the responsibility, they may never even find the courage to come forward.

Thus the first step in designing a programme among social

work, medical, legal and other agencies involves reaching a consensus on what incestuous abuse is about, and how it should be treated. That means agreeing on a theory.

If I have tried to show anything in this book, it is that decisions on how you deal with each family member depend crucially on how you theorise about them. Is he/she mad, bad, sick or inadequate; blameless, collusive, or responsible for the whole thing? Are we looking at a family pathology, a Freudian spiders' web, a legacy of patriarchy?

Theory decides whether you believe a runaway girl's story, and whether or not you send her home. It shapes what you tell the tearful mother who arrives on your doorstep. Should she be more dutiful to her incestuous husband and give up her job and social life, or should she be less obedient and dutiful? It determines the policy you design for the offender: should he be imprisoned, removed from the home, psychoanalysed, or helped to repair his marriage? It decides whether or not you intervene at all: is incest just a happy part of that culture, and best left alone?

That is why we have spent so long talking about theory. It is also why caring agencies must begin by hammering out the very basis of their policies, however time-consuming, stressful or conflictual the exercise may be.

No two countries are similar either in their problems or in the advantages they have to offer. We cannot find easy solutions by simply copying programmes from the United States or other parts of Europe. Legal and other differences even exist between England and Scotland. None the less it is very worthwhile to look at some examples of intervention and the ideas that underpin them if one is setting out to design a coherent programme.

It is also vital to remember that help, therapy or treatment, however necessary and important, is itself a sign and admission of society's failure to protect some of its most vulnerable people. We cannot forever be locking the stable door. The greatest priority is prevention and deterrence. In tackling something which wreaks so much damage and trauma, we must help create a climate where sexual abuse meets instant exposure and universal social condemnation.

Thus it is important to look not just at examples of treatment but also at campaigning and publicity work, especially where it is aimed at arming children and women with the knowledge and self confidence to reject their victimisation. This includes work in schools and through the media. It is an area where feminist groups could play a still more active part.

This section will describe some of the work done by one comprehensive project, at Harborview in Seattle, and discuss an example of legal intervention through the Children's Hearings system here in Scotland. It will mention co-operative projects between statutory and voluntary groups in the Republic of Ireland and Scotland, and look at work being done by some of the Incest Survivor Groups which have sprung up all over Britain in the last few years.

These projects have no identical philosophy. But they do make some basic assumptions. Sexual abuse is highly damaging and a misuse of power; nobody deserves to suffer it; intervention is needed; the male offender must take responsibility; his treatment must be backed with legal sanction; protection from further abuse is the priority. I must stress that while I have tried to give accurate basic information about these projects developments continually occur. Readers should check the latest situation with the organisations themselves.

Harborview

The Sexual Assault Center at Harborview was set up in 1973, as a unit within Harborview Medical Center (a university-administrated hospital, housing the main emergency room for the Seattle area). Staff include paediatricians, social workers and other specialists and there is close co-operation with law enforcement agencies. About half the sexual assault victims seen are under 16 and half of these have suffered incestuous abuse. In their 1977–79 survey of 593 children (q.v.) they found more than 22 per cent were between one and six years old.

Where abuse is known or suspected there is immediate intervention and the child and offender are separated. The child is assessed for medical and psychological needs and counselling sessions are arranged. Other children in the family are checked for sexual abuse, counselling such as a women's group is arranged for the non-offending parent, and the offender is evaluated by a qualified expert in sexual deviance.

Conditions may be agreed by a contract with the children's protective services worker or be contained in a petition to the court. There may be an agreed order or a hearing, and all parties can have a lawyer.

Where the accused denies the charge there must be no contact at all with the child till after the trial or hearing (to avoid pressure to retract, and to protect the child.) Where abuse is admitted or confirmed visits should only be when desired by the child and where the offender is in an approved treatment programme; visits are strictly supervised.

If the family intends to reunite after intervention, separation is expected to last 6-18 months. Re-entry will depend on the child's wishes and her ability to report future offence behaviour; on the mother's ability to protect the child; and on the offender's treatment progress as determined by a qualified therapist. Contact will be gradual and supervised and family counselling will be part of the process.

Through clinical experience Harborview workers have increasingly moved away from the notion that incest is a result of dysfunctional problems within a family, leading to maladaptive behaviour. Rather they believe the sexual deviancy of one member, usually the father, causes the other problems in the family. They treat sceptically the offender's claims to be cured, regard him as permanently vulnerable to re-offence, and build this into his treatment programme. The men need to change their sexual preferences, attitudes and beliefs, and uncompromisingly accept their responsibility.

Some people, including feminists, will want to question Harborview's description of child sexual preference as a deviation, especially where this involves any form of aversion therapy. They will stress how many offenders will abuse both girls and women of all ages, and will see basic attitudes to women and to male/female sexuality as the primary problem. None the less the sceptical view of the male offender, backed by long clinical experience, means an important input into a treatment debate characterised by over-optimism and complacency has emerged via research papers that should be a must on agencies' reading lists.

Likewise Harborview have produced detailed and high-quality papers on designing counselling programmes for older and younger children at different stages of therapy; for mothers, and mothers and children. Comprehensive checklists for spotting sexual abuse, and detailed programmes on organising contacts between offenders and families, are also available. Harborview lay great stress on preventive work and a large-scale publicity programme includes talks in schools and peak-hour TV programmes. They have claimed that there is not a child in Seattle who is unaware of their project.

The law can protect children: examples from Scotland

By itself, the best law in the world cannot protect children from sexual abuse. They and their families have to feel able to report it in the first place. But even when this happens today, survivors face huge problems with the legal system: long delays, with all the pressures to retract; a court atmosphere that frightens or confuses younger children, whose testimony is in any case dubiously regarded; scepticism towards teenage girls, with aggressive or offensive questioning by defence lawyers; all the problems of corroboration for acts which by their nature take place in secret.

But though wider legal reforms are still much needed, the Children's Hearings system in Scotland could begin to react swiftly and effectively to incestuous abuse, according to Peter Ferguson, who has been encouraging this course as depute Reporter in Highland Region.

Peter Ferguson, who believes a high level of intervention within a legal framework is essential to protect the child, points out that of 937 incest cases reported to police in Scotland between 1951 and 1978 only 347 were prosecuted and 285 defendants were convicted. Such cases can take up to a year to come to court. But there is no problem in fitting abusive behaviour within the conditions for referral to a hearing.

Early referral to a hearing means compulsory measures of care may be invoked quickly and that, if the abuse is not admitted, the Reporter can bring a 'diet of proof' before a sheriff, which must begin within 28 days. The standard of proof is the civil one, the 'balance of probabilities' while applications are held in private and in less formal settings, which helps children give their evidence calmly and clearly. Unlike the courts, the Reporters may compel a wife to attend and give evidence.

The Reporter cannot be prevented from leading evidence about the accused man's sexual history if this is relevant. Further, in these hearings 'most solicitors appear constrained to avoid such vigorous attacks upon child witnesses as would be mounted in the criminal court.'

Reporters, who are committed to the welfare of children, should increase their skills on the subject of sexual abuse, says Peter Ferguson: getting evidence from children is a skill to be developed, not only on the basics, like what slang a child uses, but in breaking new ground, perhaps by the use of anatomically correct dolls in court. Use of specialists to give expert evidence should also be increased.

But he believes that while hearings can and should be used for speedy protection of incest victims, the abusers should still be prosecuted in the criminal courts. The two main changes necessary involve speeding up proceedings and reforming the archaic rule that one spouse cannot be made to give evidence against another.

The vital role of teachers

Teachers spend more time with children and teenagers than any other professional group. For abused children the school, where they spend six or seven hours a day, is in a sense the main refuge from their most threatening and assaultive environment. Teachers have unique opportunities to do two things: to pick up the signs of abuse and initiate action to protect the child; and to take part in preventive education, encouraging children to protect and defend themselves by arming them with knowledge.

Yet for many adult survivors, ten years or more of their lives passed without them feeling able to tell their secret to teachers, or without being believed when they did. Clearly schools are still a very long way from offering the environment abused children need to break their confidences in safety. But teachers cannot be expected, with sighs of relief from the rest of us, to shoulder the tasks of exposure, counselling and prevention single handed. Already overburdened and with a growing sense that they are expected to tackle every social and educational problem pupils face, they have a right to expect support and resources from other agencies if they are to play a major part in identifying and preventing incestuous abuse.

But it is important at this stage that concerned and committed teachers take the initiative in persuading their colleagues, in the school and in their unions, that involvement in tackling sexual abuse should be a priority for the profession, particularly for guidance and psychology staff, with the backing of the classroom teacher's close knowledge and observation of pupils in their care. That means starting to speak out about their experience and beliefs at every level and asking for backing for a coherent policy from education administrators in local authorities.

Women teachers in some British schools have already struggled, some successfully, to promote a 'whole-school' policy on dealing with sexual abuse. This includes getting staff to talk about their own prejudices and experience; ensuring teachers are familiar with some of the signs and symptoms of abuse; adopting principles, for instance that children should be believed; making discussion of sexual abuse part of sex education courses.

Teachers, even within one school, may find themselves unable to agree on the ethical and practical problems of breaking a pupil's confidence and informing other agencies. But even the debate itself is likely to improve awareness and sensitivity, and lead to demands on legal and social work agencies for support and co-ordinated action.

The majority of the teaching profession in Britain is female. Not the most powerful section, but perhaps a strong enough one to force a concealed yet mainly female experience on to the public agenda. Social workers, psychiatrists, health visitors and police regularly take part in conferences or seminars on incestuous abuse: teachers are more reticent, or perhaps people forget to invite them. A well-publicised day conference, perhaps jointly sponsored by several unions, would be one way of enabling teachers to speak out forcefully about their own experience and anxieties.

Teachers also have a key role in prevention programmes, which have been far more familiar and widely used in the USA and in other countries than here. But Michele Elliott, a leading worker in this field, believes teachers and education authorities can overestimate the problems of persuading parents that their children should be give open and frank warnings about sexual abuse.

In school pilot schemes with her 'Kidscape' programme she found the project could hardly meet the demand and that virtually 100 per cent of parents agreed their children could take part. The project, which uses a variety of teaching aids for parents, pupils and teachers, aims to offer children practical ways of keeping safe from sexual assault.

This includes bringing home the difference between loving affection and forced or tricked intimacy; telling them what secrets should not be kept; teaching simple rules of safety at home and in the streets; advising parents how to spot signs of abuse and how to respond if their child confesses abuse. Drama, role play and videos are also used in the schools.

'Kidscape', which operates from 82 Brook Street in London , has teaching packs for 5–11 year olds and is preparing others for older and younger children, along with training kits for teachers, social workers and others involved in the care of young people.

Informing each other: women's groups and statutory agencies

One major problem about tackling social abuses which mainly affect women has been mutual suspicion, sometimes even hostility, between feminist groups and statutory agencies like the police, medical or social services. The gulf in ideology which often exists over how to tackle the problems can be widened by unhappy experiences of contact. Radically different 'solutions' to abuses can co-exist in the same area. Often women's groups which are branded extreme or anti-men struggle on little or no official funding to give a voluntary service on which women may make heavy demands.

Organisations like Women's Aid or Rape Crisis Centres (RCC) have had different experiences of co-operation in different parts of the country, and must have the right to decide their own policies on this. Two examples can be given here of RCCs which have set out actively to inform and persuade statutory groups about their approach to sexual abuse, and to co-operate with them on projects.

Strathclyde RCC

Strathclyde RCC found the number of calls made to them increased sharply between 1978 and 1981, with up to 50 per cent relating to incestuous abuse. Many calls came from the East End of Glasgow where the RCC had already worked informally with agencies like social work, community education and the police.

They applied for and received, via Strathclyde Region, Urban Aid funding for a pilot scheme called the Women's Support Project, based in the East End. The aim was to work with local groups (statutory and voluntary) to develop a co-ordinated, informed service for women and girls who were sexually assaulted.

They employed two development workers, one to work with young women and girls in the area. They sought to raise awareness of rape and sexual abuse against women and children and provide a forum for discussion on the subject. They held information sessions for groups like health visitors and community psychiatric nurses and put together an information pack which agencies could use for work with young girls. They publicised services available to women throughout the area.

They also helped develop local self-help groups to break down the isolation many women and girls feel after sexual assault.

The Women's Support Project, in collaboration with Women's Aid, have also run two training days highlighting the causal factor of male violence in incestuous abuse and domestic violence. They hoped this would encourage a consistent positive approach from the whole range of agencies which abused women and children turn to for help.

Invitations included health centres and GPs; police, housing offices, local schools; community education and social work.

Workshops, role play and videos were used and workers were encouraged to draw on their own life experiences to help them understand crises faced by abused women. A wide range of leaflets, research papers and statistical material was available. Invitations were open to women and men, though few men attended on either day.

Strathclyde RCC believes such sessions also give support and encouragement to workers in statutory groups who feel isolated in their feminist views and who are concerned about attitudes to women which they hear expressed in their own agencies. From attendance at one of the days it was clear that many sympathetic and interested workers from across the range of official groups were not just hungry for information, but were also able to give the women's groups many insights into their own work and problems.

For instance one male social worker described how he was expected both to prepare a report on an incestuous father and to counsel the teenage girl involved. He found this professionally and personally stressful and did not feel he was the right person to counsel the girl. He successfully persuaded his superiors to provide her with a female social worker, but only after much resistance.

Dublin RCC

Women and girls have faced many problems in the Irish Republic where divorce and abortion are banned, contraceptive services are severly restricted, and where open discussion of sexual matters meets social and religious constraints in many parts of the country. Yet sexual abuse and sexual problems are widespread, as books like Rosita Sweetman's *On our Backs* have graphically shown. Well-publicised legal cases like the 'Kerry Babies' gave insights into the pressures facing unmarried pregnant women, which shocked many people in Ireland as well as beyond it.

But the Irish Republic also has a strong and vocal women's movement, and sections of it have won more acceptance and cooperation from official agencies than might be expected, helping to produce some initiatives which could give an example to the UK.

Dublin Rape Crisis Centre, which receives financial help from Government, has six paid staff including two qualified counsellors. In 1985, they found that 564 of their 965 calls related to incest or child sexual abuse; in the first quarter of 1986, the figure was 249 out of 363 calls. They offer short and long term counselling and run self help groups, and organise rape crisis counselling courses for women across the country.

Dublin RCC were actively involved in the setting up of the sexual assault treatment unit in Dublin's Rotunda Hospital. With other bodies including the Department of Health, they helped train and select women doctors to work in the unit.

This centre deals with medical examinations of rape and sexual assault victims in the Dublin area, and tests for forensic evidence where the Gardai (police) are involved. It gives all necessary medical treatment and advice, and refers clients to the RCC for counselling.

Dublin RCC employ a fundraiser and have gained funds through many 'orthodox' events including the Dublin City Marathon. The most striking example of mainstream co-operation comes from their extensive programme of talks and seminars. In some parts of Britain RCCs, even Women's Aid, have struggled to persuade the police to let them through the door; in the Republic (of all places?) theological colleges, convents, schools, youth clubs and youth training schemes are only a few places that have welcomed RCC speakers. Others include trade unions, health boards and social work courses.

Dublin RCC's structured day training courses include sessions on confidentiality, definitions of child sexual abuse, signs and symptoms, handling of disclosure, the role of youth leaders, and discussions of personal feelings and experiences.

Dublin RCC are also represented on another major Irish project run by the Irish Council for Civil Liberties (ICCL). In late 1984 the ICCL was awarded a £25,000 grant by the Department of Health to carry out research into the nature and extent of child sexual abuse in the Irish Republic, to identify treatment available and to make recommendations about the training of voluntary and statutory agencies. The working party, which includes Senator Mary Robinson, also aims to produce a comprehensive legal report.

In addition ICCL has produced an information pack on child sexual abuse which includes contact addresses for help, statistics, indicators of abuse, indirect signals children may give, personal accounts of abuse, 'myths and facts', and notes on the legal situation in Ireland.

Scottish Action Against Incest

In the last few years, self-help groups of 'incest survivors' – mainly adult women have sprung up all over Britain. Many of these developed via rape crisis centres which almost universally found an upsurge of calls relating to incestuous abuse. Abuse which often happened twenty or more years earlier in a woman's life. The ethos of the groups is that women can only recover from the experience and rebuild their self worth through taking control of their own lives. Many women who take part have already had disillusioning experiences with professionals, especially psychiatrists.

A number of Scottish survivor groups, (there are six at present), have come together with rape crisis centres in a loose federation, Scottish Action Against Incest (SAAI). Founded in 1983, SAAI aims to provide free confidential services for abused women and children, put mothers in touch with each other, encourage research into prevention of abuse, and educate and inform the public.

Local voluntary groups have found they have had to concentrate resources on intensive counselling with individuals and groups. Due to an overwhelming demand on their services (including incest crisis 'phone lines at RCCs) they have been able to launch little in the way of publicity, campaigning and educational work, or to maintain effective links between groups.

Their national conference in 1985 therefore resolved to explore ways of employing paid workers. These would aim to give survivors a voice to help break the taboo of silence surrounding incest, and provide statutory and voluntary groups with knowledge and training.

SAAI have established contact with various organisations including major hospitals, local social work departments, Strathclyde Police, and Glasgow housing department.

SAAI are also campaigning for legal changes. One of their leading workers, Kathy Kerr, has urged consideration of the Israeli system where an 'interrogator' is appointed to safeguard a child's interests before and during court proceedings. They can speak for the child and make sure she is not harassed in court. Taped evidence from the child is also admitted.

Scottish Women's Aid have also taken a keen interest in the problems of incestuous abuse. In 1983, the Scottish Women's Aid Incest Group based in Dundee produced a special information pack an incest, which was sponsored by Tayside Regional Council.

Incest survivors campaign (ISC)

Set up in 1981 and run as a collective by and for women, the ISC has had a substantial influence both as a focus for new survivor groups that were set up across the country, and as a radical force in publicly challenging traditional definitions and treatment. Leading members, in particular Emily Driver, have been active in speaking at conferences and meetings throughout the UK, and while the ISC's uncompromising and confrontational style has been hard for some professionals and others to accept, it must take credit for forcing many people into a painful reassessment of the assumptions they have worked with for many years.

The ISC's aims have included educating the public and improving legal and social services for abused women and girls; putting survivors in touch with each other; supporting mothers; encouraging foundation of groups; doing research and contributing articles; founding refuges for girls; running newsletters; making international contacts.

Problems including funding difficulties and a ceaseless flow of inquiries from women put a brake on some of these developments. But ISC's activities have included monitoring the media, and taking part in TV and radio programmes; carrying out a wide ranging survey of the experience of incest survivors (1983); picketing, with leaflets, stickers and posters, films like *Butterfly*, in which a young girl seduced her father; sitting in on incest cases at court and making their presence known. They have also produced a wide range of information material including detailed check lists on the signs and symptoms of sexual abuse.

In September 1984 ISC set up the Child Sexual Abuse Preventive Education Project (CSAPEP) and a year later obtained a GLC grant which enabled them to employ six workers. Since abolition of the GLC they have been trying to secure new funding.

CSAPEP has produced leaflets for children, mothers and teenagers and do consultations with teachers, individually and in groups. Their success in getting into schools to give talks has been limited so far. They run workshops for professionals and their paid workers developed training courses. They are keen both to move into community education and to act as consultants to local social work units and children's homes, but stress they need more funding and a larger workforce to do these things efficiently.

Conclusion

In the last few years there have been many hopeful developments in society's approach to incestuous abuse. Most important, as we have seen in this section, women themselves have demanded that their voices be heard. They have said unequivocally: this happened to thousands of us; we neither invited, enjoyed nor colluded in it; we suffered a monstrous injustice which scarred our whole lives; we demand a say in how we repair our lives, and in the action you take to confront this injustice in future.

Largely as a result of that pressure, incestuous abuse is slowly being recognised as a major social problem. Professional agencies have been forced to ask themselves what they should be doing about it, and some of them have been encouraged to question their lifelong assumptions about the meaning, causes and treatment of 'incest'. Most are now far more reluctant to indulge in overt 'victim blame', or to deny that the abuse has damaging effects.

There has also been grudging acceptance of the need for self help groups and facilities which are independent of professional 'experts'. This is a considerable advance, especially if it is backed by official funding for projects. But as groups like Women's Aid are aware, it can have dangers too: for official agencies can be tempted to refer people to voluntary agencies with a sigh of relief, instead of tackling seriously their own need to make a response.

But overall, there has been far more progress on the need for 'repair jobs' than on the urgent need for prevention. Successful prevention means accepting unpalatable analyses of what is wrong in the first place, and any message that reads 'abuse of male power' has proved remarkably indigestible and unacceptable throughout history.

Take the Women's Aid experience again: they have won much public sympathy for the plight of battered women, and support for refuges – for the bandaging job. Yet 15 years on from the first upsurge of activity in this country, Women's Aid have made little headway in getting society to accept that violence against women is, in the words of Rebecca and Russell Dobash, 'an extension of cultural misogyny' which will only be prevented by major changes in social attitudes, in male and female socialisation, and in a shift of power towards women within the family. There is no evidence at all that domestic violence has been reduced. The warning is there.

Where incest is concerned, many assumptions are being swept away by the tide. Yet professionals cling to the collusive wife theory like drowning men grasping at flotsam. Could it be because it is such a powerful defence against admitting the male abuse of power? And because without it family therapists might be like emperors without clothes? These are harsh questions which they owe it to their own integrity to ask.

The new sense of urgency among official agencies about child sexual abuse is more than welcome. Likewise incest survivor groups and crisis lines are vital: they also contribute crucially to making women's voices, and women's protest, heard so that it can no longer be silenced or ignored. But we must also direct our energies to the task of uncompromising campaigning on what sexual abuse is about, we must keep pressing professionals to discard the comfortable theories which only prolong self-deception and unchecked abuse, we must campaign for legal changes, and for the education of children, however young, so that they can speak out and be believed.

We must help create a climate where incestuous abuse will not be worth the risk, so that people do not have to spend their energies repairing the damage again and again after it is done. It is a selfish, squalid and premeditated crime which can have no justification or excuse. We should at the least not collude in the unremitting efforts of powerful people to provide those excuses.

Appendix 1: Preventive work with children

Many adults who want to make children more aware of the dangers of sexual abuse in general, and incestuous abuse in particular, worry about the most appropriate ways to do this without producing over-anxiety in children. There are also concerns about how the subject can be made 'acceptable' to parents, local authorities, media chiefs and establishment agencies generally whose permission may be needed for publicity. Where there is still controversy about sex education in schools, many teachers who want to play a role in preventing and detecting incestuous abuse may particularly need advice on this.

This section gives some examples of work being done in this area. The first is an extract from the text of a simple leaflet for older primary school children, designed by the Child Sexual Abuse Preventive Education Project (CSAPEP) in London. It is important to point out that they hold the copyright for this. The full text, along with other leaflets for younger children and for teenagers, is available from the CSAPEP or from the Information Service on Incest and Child Sexual Abuse. (Both addresses given in Appendix 2.)

The Information Service also provides lists of recommended videos and books for children on resisting child sexual abuse. Some of these are listed below. The National Society For The Prevention Of Cruelty To Children (NSPCC) produce a reading list of books on child sexual abuse prevention from their Headley Library and can be contacted direct for further information.

Finally, many groups and agencies are starting to produce guidelines on detecting child sexual abuse. One example of this is the Survivor Alert List produced by the Incest Survivors Campaign (ISC). It is available from: ISC, c/o A Woman's Place, Hungerford House, Victoria Embankment, London WC2. I am particularly indebted to Rasjidah St John for help with this section.

Extract From *It's Your Body* (CSAPEP)

Your body belongs to *you*
Sometimes you can know someone for a long time and like them a lot and then they'll start to do things you don't like at all. Perhaps they'll start touching you in a way that seems strange to you, but since you like the person and he's always been nice to you, you don't like to ask him to stop. But you can and you should. Because you don't have to let anyone touch you in a way you don't like, even if it's an adult you've always got on well with. Or even if it's someone in your own family, or a neighbour.

Strangers
You've probably been told many times not to take sweets from strangers, or get into a car with someone you don't know, because they might do bad things to you. But people we know well can also do bad things to us, by making us believe they are *not* bad.

It's unfair if a grown-up makes you do things you don't understand
In fact the grownup (or sometimes it's a teenager) is being very unfair, because he is bigger than you and knows more about everything. So he can easily get you to do things you don't really want to. So that later on, when you *do* understand, you'll feel very ANGRY. I'm saying 'he' all the time, but it can sometimes be a woman.

Remember, it's *your* body, and you can say '*NO*'.

Find someone who can help you
If you can't get the person to stop bothering you and you can't keep out of his way, you should tell someone you think will help … a schoolteacher, or your mother, or an older sister, or a policewoman for instance. If you tell one person and they don't believe you, or are too frightened to help you, then try someone else. Keep trying till you find someone who *will* help. Also, tell your friends. Then they'll know to stay away from that person too, and maybe their parents can help.

You are not to blame
It *is* frightening when something like this happens. But you can be sure that it's all right to say 'NO'. And you can be sure, too, that it's not your fault. It's nothing *you've* done that made this person behave the way he did. He has probably done it to other children.

And he will most likely go on doing it unless we make sure he can't. We don't like telling tales, but this is different. Especially when someone threatens you with all sorts of nasty things if you tell ... that is *blackmail*. You know then that it's not a secret you should keep. If you tell people, he can be stopped.

ISICSA recommended videos on incest and child abuse

Kids Can Say No!
Rolf Harris Video, 1985, 20 minutes. Ages 5–11.
Children talk about kinds of touch they like and kinds they don't. Four well chosen incidents are acted and children discuss what happened, how it might have been avoided and what to do if something did happen. Everyone sings 'My body's nobody's body but mine' with gusto. Forthright and determined, very well done.
From: Rolf Harris Video, 43 Drury Lane, London WC2B 5RT Tel. 01 240 8777 Price £36.00 inc. VAT. Can be hired: £8 for five days from: Central Film Library, Chalfont Grove, Gerrards Cross, Bucks SL9 8TN

Touch
Cordelia Anderson and the Illusion Theater Co. USA. 1983, 32 minutes.
Children offer ideas on good touch, bad touch and confusing touch; actors play incidents involving different kinds of touch and verbal and other forms of abuse; all discuss ways of preventing and stopping abuse. Excellent for children, teachers, parents and all workers in this field.
From: Guild Sound and Vision, 6 Royce Road, Peterborough PE1 5YB Tel. 0733 315 315 Price £78.00 inc. VAT and P&P.

No More Secrets
Jennifer Fay and Caren Adams (authors of the book of the same title) USA, 1982. 13 minutes. Ages 8–13.
Four children help each other with advice on how to stop sexual abuse. 'Tell him, really *tell* him, not to do it'. Some animation also. A very attractive film. Price £75.00 plus VAT.

Feeling Yes, Feeling No
Four videos, Canadian.
Parts 1, 2 and 3 for use with children aged 6–14, each part 15 minutes. A catchy song 'My body's nobody's body but mine', and

three easy stranger rules. Part 4 for teachers and parents, 28 minutes; five easy rules for listening to children. £160.00 plus VAT. Can be hired at £20.00 plus VAT.

The above two videos are available from: Educational Media International, 25 Boileau Road, London W5 3AL Tel. 01 998 8657

ISICSA recommended books on resisting sexual abuse

No is not enough: helping teenagers avoid sexual assault
Adams, Caren et al (Impact Publishers, USA, 1984) £5.95. A parents' guide. Also good for teenagers themselves to read.

I like you to make jokes with me, but I don't want you to touch me
Bass, Ellen and Betz, Marti (Lollipop Power Inc., USA, 1981) £2.70. How a four year old learns to tell the grocer on what terms she is prepared to be his friend. Lots of pictures.

No more secrets for me
Wachter, Oralee (Penguin, 1986) £1.95.
Four good stories with black and white pictures by Caroline Binch. For children aged 7–11. Stories illustrate what a child's rights are, what situations might be risky, how to prevent sexual abuse, and what to do if you are abused. The first British book.

It's my body: a book to teach young children how to resist uncomfortable touch
Freeman, Lory (Parenting Press, Inc., Seattle, USA, 1982) £3.00.
A lovely book with pictures, for reading aloud to pre-school children, age 2–5, with phrases eg. 'Don't do that!' for them to practice saying as if 'they really mean it'.

Top secret: sexual assault information for teenagers only
Fay, Jennifer and Flerchinger, B. (King County Rape Relief, Renton, USA, 1982) £3.00.
An attractive book in pop format and graphics imparting good information and advice in a 'can't put it down' style.

It's O.K. to say no: activity book
Smith, Frank (Peter Haddock, UK, 1985) 79p from W. H. Smith.
Games, puzzles, pictures to colour in, mazes, all showing children how to protect themselves against sexual assault by people they know as well as strangers.

It's O.K. to say no: colouring book
Smith, Frank (Peter Haddock, UK, 1985) 79p from W. H. Smith.
Pictures to colour in, for four year olds upwards, with explanatory
text adult can read aloud explaining how children can protect
themselves from sexual assault.

Appendix 2: Contacts

Sexual abuse centres in the British Isles

Scotland

Aberdeen Rape Crisis Centre, P.O. Box 123, Aberdeen Tel.
0224 575560
Mon. 6pm–8pm Thurs. 7pm–9pm (answerphone)

Aberdeen Incest Survivors Group, c/o Aberdeen Rape Crisis
Centre

Central Scotland Rape Crisis Centre, P.O. Box 4, Falkirk Tel.
0324 38433

Central Scotland Incest Survivors Group c/o Central Scotland
Rape Crisis Centre

Central Scotland Action Against Incest c/o Central Scotland Rape
Crisis Centre

Dundee Rape Crisis Line, P.O. Box 83, Dundee Tel. 0382 646377
Wed. 7–9pm.

Dundee Incest Survivors Group c/o Dundee Women's Aid, 22
Thomson Street, Dundee

Dundee Action Against Incest c/o Dundee Rape Crisis Line.

Dunfermline Rape Crisis Line, PO Box 47, Dunfermline Tel.
0383 739084.
Fri. 7–9pm.

Edinburgh Rape Crisis Centre, P.O. Box 120, Edinburgh Tel.
031 556 9437.
Mon. 12–2pm, 6–8pm, Tues.6–8pm, Thur. 7–10pm, Fri. 6–8pm.

Edinburgh Incest Survivors Group, c/o Edinburgh Rape Crisis
Centre   Survivors Line 031 556 9437.
Wed. 6–8pm.

Edinburgh Action Against Incest c/o 61a Broughton Street,
Edinburgh

Highland Rape Crisis and Counselling Line c/o IVOG, 38
Ardconnel Street, Inverness Tel. 0463 220719.
Sat. and Sun. 7–10pm.

Kirkaldy Incest Survivors Group c/o The Volunteer Centre, 18
Brycedale Avenue, Kirkaldy Tel. 0592 204756.

Strathclyde Rape Crisis Centre, P.O. Box 53, Glasgow G21 YR
Tel. 041 221 8448.
Mon., Wed., Fri. 7pm–10pm

Glasgow Incest Survivors Group c/o Strathclyde Rape Crisis
Centre

Glasgow Action Against Incest c/o 48 Miller Street, Glasgow

England
Avon Sexual Abuse Centre c/o Bristol RCL, 39 Jamaica St, Stokes
Croft, Bristol BS2 8JP Tel. Bristol 428331
Mon–Fri. 10.30am–2.30pm
Bristol Incest Survivors have their own magazine, *Taboo*, a highly
professional production which may interest many other groups.

Birmingham Rape Crisis, P.O. Box 558, Birmingham B3 2HL Tel.
021 233 2122
24 hour service

Cambridge Incest Survivors c/o Cambridge RCC, Box R, 12 Mill
Road, Cambridge Tel. Cambridge 358314
Wed. 6pm–12 midnight, Sat. 11am–5pm

Coventry: One In Four, Box 8, c/o Coventry Voluntary Services Council, 28 Corporation Street, Coventry CV1 1AB Tel. Coventry 76606
Tuesdays 11am–3pm.

Grays Thurrock RCC, Bridge House, 160 Bridge Road, Grays Thurrock, Essex RM17 6DB Tel. Grays Thurrock 380609
Mon. 6pm–9pm, Tues. 7pm–10pm, Wed. 1pm–5pm, Thurs. 12 midday–4pm
Women's group and individual counselling.

Harlow Incest Survivors Group and Crisis Line, Women's Centre, 93–96 Altham Grove, Harlow, Essex Tel. Harlow 21612
Group meets Tues. 8pm–10pm. Crisis line open Tues. morning and Wed. evening. It is understood that this is not a feminist group.

London:

Child Sexual Abuse Preventive Education Project (CSAPEP) c/o AWP, Hungerford House, Victoria Embankment, London WC2N 6PA Tel. 01 671 9033

Incest Survivors Campaign c/o A Woman's Place, Hungerford House, Victoria Embankment, London WC2N 6PA Tel. 01 671 9033

Information Service on Incest and Child Sexual Abuse (ISICSA), 24 Blackheath Rise, London SE13 7PN Tel. 01 852 7432

Kingston Women's Centre, 66 London Road, Kingston-on-Thames, Surrey Tel. 01 541 1964
Women's group and girls group.

Lambeth Incest Survivors, South London Women's Centre, 55 Acre Lane, Brixton, London SW2 Tel. 01 274 7215
Drop-in every Tues. 11am–12.30pm

London Rape Crisis Line, P.O. Box 69, London WC1X 9NJ Tel. 01 837 1600
24 hour service.

Waltham Forest Incest Survivors c/o Waltham Forest Women's Centre, 109 Hoe Street, London E17 Tel. 01 520 5318

Women's Advice and Counselling Service, The Albany, Douglas Way, Deptford, London SE8 Tel. 01 692 6268

Manchester

Taboo, P.O. Box 38, Manchester M60 1HG Tel. 061 236 1323
Crisis line (061 236 1712) Wed. 4pm–8.30pm

Sheffield Incest Survivors group c/o Sheffield Rape Crisis Line, P.O. Box 34, Sheffield S1 1UD Tel. 0742 755255
Mon.–Fri. 11am–4pm, Tues. 7.30pm–9.30pm, Thurs. 7pm–9pm

Sussex Incest Crisis Line c/o Brighton Rape Crisis Project, P.O. Box 332, Hove, East Sussex Tel. Brighton 24316

Eire

Dublin Rape Crisis, 2 Lower Pembroke Street, Dublin 2 Tel. Dublin 601 470
Mon.–Fri. 8pm–8am, Sat./Sun. 24 hours.
Individual counselling and self-help groups.

Northern Ireland

Belfast Rape Crisis Centre, P.O. Box 46, Belfast BT2 7AR Tel. Belfast 249696
Mon.–Fri. 10am–6pm, Sat. and Sun. 11am–5pm.

Mothers

Chris Strickland Tel. 0965 31432.

For men

London

Incest Crisis Line, Richard Tel. 01 388 2388
ISICSA lists the Incest Crisis Line as 'for men'. However, the line is open to survivors of both sexes and the counsellors involved are both male and female.

Sheffield

SMASH (Sheffield Men Against Sexual Harassment), P.O. Box 281, Sheffield 1HN Tel. Sheffield 584643

For local contacts in other areas and centres in other countries write to ISICSA (address given above).

Other useful contacts

Standing Committee on Sexual Abuse of Children, Crown House, London Rd, Morden, Surrey SM4 5DX

National Society for the Prevention of Cruelty to Children (includes Headley Library), 67 Saffron Hill, London EC1 N8RS

Royal Scottish Society for Prevention of Cruelty to Children, 41 Polwarth Terrace, Edinburgh EH 11

Also RSSPCC, Overnewton Centre, 52 Lumsden Street, Glasgow G3 8RH; and RSSPCC (Ms Alice Sheridan and Mr Sam McTaggart) 15 Annifield Place, Glasgow. They work with abused children and mothers, and plan to open an Incest Crisis 'phone line'.

British Association for the Study and Prevention of Child Abuse and Neglect (BASPCAN) Hon sec: Mr A. Belford, Dept. of Reporter to the Children's Panel, 91 Commercial St, Dundee.
    The Scottish branch hold regular open meetings and discussions on child sexual abuse. These have attracted a wide range of professional agencies and voluntary groups. Mr Norman Dunning, at the Overnewton Centre, can also be contacted about this programme.

BASPCAN (England): Hon. Sec. J. Pickett, The Withens, 30 Bankfield Lane, Norden, Rochdale, Lancashire

Late entry

Childline, freephone service for children who are being physically or sexually abused. Tel. 0800 1111.

Appendix 3:
broken silences

Folk songs (many of which were probably written by women) reveal many of the abuses, sufferings and injustices faced by women over the centuries. But though the infanticide theme is common, there are very few songs indeed about incest. Even through this medium, the silence was rarely broken.

The remarkable song produced below is not hard to find: it is reproduced in a number of books and records. But it is widely dismissed by commentators as a fantastic flight of imagination, or 'a gruesome story, belonging to the moral-carrying body of ballads and even fairy-tales of mediaeval days'. On the contrary, its horror has a realistic ring.

Recently a woman in her thirties, who grew up in a rural area of Ireland, confessed to a researcher that before she was thirteen she gave birth to two children, one by her father and one by a farm labourer. The children were smothered at birth by her mother, who had delivered them.

The Well below the Valley

A gentleman was passing by, he asked a drink as he got
  dry
At this well below the valley-o.

chorus:
Green grows the lily-o, right among the bushes-o.

She said 'My cup it overflows, if I stoop down I might fall
  in
At the well below the valley-o.

If your true love was passing by, you'd fill him a drink if
  he got dry
At the well below the valley-o.

She swore by grass, she swore by corn, that her true
  love was never born
At the well below the valley-o.

I say, young maid, you're swearing wrong, for five fine
  children you had born
At the well below the valley-o.

If you're a man of noble fame, you'll tell me who's the
  father of them
At the well below the valley-o.

There was two of them by your uncle Dan, another two
  by your brother John
At the well below the valley-o.

Another by your father dear at the well below the valley-
  o
At the well below the valley-o.

Well if you're a man of noble fame, you'll tell me what did
  happen to them
At the well below the valley-o.

There was two of them buried by the stable door,
  another two 'neath the kitchen floor
At the well below the valley-o.

Another's buried by the well, at the well below the
  valley-o
At the well below the valley-o.

Well if you're a man of noble fame, you'll tell me what will
  happen myself
At the well below the valley-o.

You'll be seven years a-portering in hell, and seven
  years a-ringing a bell
At the well below the valley-o.

I'll be seven years a-ringing a bell, but the Lord above
  may save my soul from portin' in hell
At the well below the valley-o.

Bibliography

This is not a comprehensive bibliography of an extensive and growing literature on incest and child sexual abuse. It is a checklist and acknowledgement of references contained in the text. It also includes examples of major research and other work done in recent years.

ANGELOU, MAYA *I know why the caged bird sings* (Virago, 1983) Autobiography.

ARMSTRONG, L. *Kiss daddy goodnight: a speakout on incest* (Pocket Books, New York, 1978)

BAKER, A. W. 'Child sexual abuse: a study of prevalence in Great Britain' *CAN*, 9:4 (1985)

BASS, E. and THORNTON, L., eds. *I never told anyone* (Harper & Row, 1983)

BEEZLEY MRAZEK, P. and KEMPE, H., eds. *Sexually abused children and their families* (Pergamon, 1980)

BENDER, L. and BLAU, A. 'The reaction of children to sexual relations with adults' *American Journal of Orthopsychiatry*, 7:4 (1937)

BENTOVIM, A. 'How prevalent is sexual abuse of children in the community, what are its consequences and how should we respond legally and therapeutically?' *Association of Child Psychology and Psychiatry Newsletter*, 6:2 (1984)

BERLINER, L. and ERNST, E. *Group treatment with pre-adolescent sexual assault survivors*
What to expect from the children's protective services
Visitation and contact
Sexual abuse of children – the offender
All the above available from: Child Sexual Abuse Clinical Consultation Group, Harborview Medical Center, 325 Ninth Avenue, Seattle, Washington 98104 USA

BENWARD, J. and DENSEN-GERBER, J. 'Incest as a causative

factor in anti-social behaviour: an exploratory study' *Contemporary Drug Problems*, 4 (autumn 1975)

BRITISH ASSOCIATION FOR THE STUDY AND PREVENTION OF CHILD ABUSE AND NEGLECT *Child Sexual Abuse* (BASPCAN, 1981) Available from: BASPCAN, 4 Nordale Park, Norden, Rochdale, Lancs. OL12 5RS

BROWNING, D. and BOATMAN, B. 'Incest: Children at risk' *American Journal of Psychiatry*, 134:1 (Jan. 1977)

BROWNMILLER, S. *Against our Will: men, women and rape* (Simon and Schuster, New York, 1975)

BUTLER, S. *Conspiracy of silence: the trauma of incest* (New Glide, San Francisco, 1978)
'Incest: whose reality, whose theory?' *Aegis* (summer/autumn 1980)

CAVALLIN, H. 'Incestuous fathers: a clinical report' *American Journal of Psychiatry*, 10 (1966)

CORMIER, B., KENNEDY, M. and SANGOWICZ, J. 'Psychodynamics of father–daughter incest' *Canadian Psychiatric Association Journal*, 7:5 (1962)

DIETZ, C. and CRAFT, J. 'Family dynamics of incest: a new perspective' *Social Casework* (Dec. 1980)

DOBASH, R. E. and DOBASH, R. *Violence against Wives, a case against the patriarchy* (Open Books, London, 1980)
'Science & social action: the case of wife beating' *Journal of family issues*, 2:4 (Dec. 1981)

DRIEBLATT, I. *Issues in the evaluation of the sex offender* (Washington State Psychological Association, 1982) Available from: Pacific Psychological Services, Seattle, Washington, USA

DRIVER, E. 'Incest and the role of the professional' Paper delivered to Child Abuse Symposium, Teeside Polytechnic, Middlesbrough 1984

DUBLIN RAPE CRISIS CENTRE *Annual Report 1984–85. Effective counselling strategies & some counselling issues* Both available from: Dublin RCC, 2 Lower Pembroke Street, Dublin 2

DUNNING, N. 'Child sexual abuse: BASPCAN open meetings in Scotland' *The Scottish Child* 6 (1985)

EBNER, A. 'Inzest' *Kriminalistische Abhandlungen*, 11 (1937)

ENNEW, J. *The sexual exploitation of children* (Polity, 1986)

FERENCZI, S. 'Confusion of tongues between adults and the child' *International Journal of Psycho Analysis* (1949)

FERGUSON, P. 'Child sexual abuse – can the legal system cope?' *The Scottish Child* 6 (1985) Part II Issue 7 (1985)

FINKELHOR, D. *Sexually victimized children* (Free Press, 1979)
'Sex among siblings: A survey report on its prevalence, variety

and effects' *Archives of sexual behaviour* vol. 9

'Risk factors in the sexual victimization of children' *Child Abuse and Neglect* 4:4 (1982)

'Sexual abuse: a sociological perspective' *Child Abuse and Neglect* 6:1 (1982)

FLUGEL, J. *The psychoanalytic study of the family* (L. and V. Woolf, London, 1926)

FORWARD, S. and BUCK, C. *Betrayal of innocence: incest and its devastation* (Pelican, 1981)

de FRANCIS, V. *Protecting the child victim of sex crimes committed by adults* (American Humane Association Children's Division, Denver, 1969)

FREUD, S. *The origins of psychoanalysis: letters to Wilhelm Fliess, drafts and notes* (Basic Books, New York, 1954)

GIARETTO, H. 'The treatment of father–daughter incest: a psychosocial approach' *Child Today*, 5:4 (Jul./Aug. 1976)

'Humanistic treatment of father–daughter incest' *Journal of Human Psychology* 18:4 (1978)

GUTTMACHER, M. S. *Sex Offenses: The Problem, Causes and Prevention* (W. W. Norton, New York, 1951)

HALL WILLIAMS, J. 'The neglect of incest: a criminologist's view' *Medicine, Science and the Law*, 14 (1974)

HEIMS, L. and KAUFMAN, I. 'Variations on a theme of incest' *American Journal of Orthopsychiatry*, 33 (1963)

HENDERSON, D. 'Incest: a synthesis of data' *Canadian Psychiatric Association Journal*, 17 (1972)

HERMAN, J. and HIRSCHMAN, L. 'Father–daughter incest' *Signs*, 2:4 (1977)

HOPKINS, J. ed. *Perspectives on rape and sexual assault* (Harper & Row, 1984)

INCEST & RELATED OFFENCES (SCOTLAND) BILL Bill no. 150 (HMSO)

IRISH COUNCIL FOR CIVIL LIBERTIES *Information on child sexual abuse* Information Pack (ICCL, 1985)

JACKSON, S. *On The Social Construction of Female Sexuality* (Women's Research and Resources Centre, London, 1978)

JAFFE, A., DYNNESON, L. et al 'Sexual abuse of children: an epidemiological study' *American Journal of Diseases of Children*, 129:6 (1975)

JOHNSON, R. 'Incest Crisis Line' *Health Visitor* 58:7 (1985)

JUSTICE, B. and JUSTICE, R. *The Broken Taboo – Sex in the Family* (Peter Owen, 1980)

KAUFMAN, I., PECK, A. and TAGUIN, C. 'The family constellation and overt incestuous relations between father and daughter'

American Journal of Orthopsychiatry, 24 (1954)

KEMPE, R. and KEMPE, C. H. *Child Abuse* (Fontana, 1978)

KENNEDY, M. and CORMIER, B. 'Father–daughter incest: treatment of the family' *Laval Medical*, 40 (1969)

KUBO, S. 'Researches and studies on incest in Japan', *Hiroshima Journal of Medical Sciences*, 8:1 (1959)

KINSEY, A., POMFROY, W., MARTIN, C. and GEBHARD, P. *Sexual Behaviour in the Human Female* (Saunders and Co., Philadelphia, 1953)

LEWIS, M. and SARREL, P. 'Some psychological aspects of seduction, incest and rape in childhood' *Journal American Academy of Child Psychiatry*, 4:4 (1969)

LEWIS, H. *Father–daughter incest* (Harvard University Press, 1981)

LIDZ, et al. 'The interfamilial environment of schizophrenic patients – marital schism and skew' *American Journal or Orthopsychiatry*, 114 (1957)

'LIZ' 'Too afraid to speak' *The Leveller* (2–15 April, 1982)

LUKIANOWICZ, N. 'Incest: Paternal incest, II, Other types of incest' *British Journal of Psychiatry*, 120 (Mar. 1972)

LUSTIG, N. et al. 'Incest' *Archives of General Psychiatry*, 14:1 (1966)

MACHOTKA, P. et al. 'Incest as a family affair' *Family Process*, 6 (Mar. 1967)

MACLEOD, J. *Incest and sexual abuse of children* (Women's Support Project, Glasgow, 1986)

MAISCH, H. *Incest* translated from the German by Colin Bearne (Deutsch, 1973)

MALINOWSKI, B. *Sex and Repression in Savage Society* (Routledge and Kegan Paul, 1927)

MALMQUIST, et al. 'Personality characteristics of women with repeated illegitimacies – descriptive aspects' *American Journal or Orthopsychiatry*, 36:3 (1966)

MARMOR, J. 'Orality in the hysterical personality' *Journal of American Psychoanalytic Association*, 1 (1955)

MASON, J. 'What is wrong with incest?' *SCOLAG Bulletin*, 47 (1980)

'1567 and all that' *Scots Law Times* (Dec. 1981)

MASSON, J. *The assault on truth* (Faber, 1984)

McINTYRE, K. 'The role of mothers in father–daughter incest: a feminist perspective' *Social Work* 26:6 (1981)

MEISELMANN, K. *Incest: a psychological study of causes and effects with treatment recommendations* (Jossey-Bass, 1978)

MIDDLETON, A. Review of Justice, B. and Justice, R. *The Scots-*

man, 17/5/80

MILLER, A. *Thou shalt not be aware: society's betrayal of the child* (Pluto, 1985)

MARKET & OPINION RESEARCH INTERNATIONAL *Child abuse: research study on behalf of: Gamble & Milne* Conducted Sept. 1984 (MORI, 1984)

MRAZEK, P., LYNCH, M. and BENTOVIM, A. 'Sexual abuse of children in the UK' *Child Abuse and Neglect* 7:2 (1983)

MULDOON, L., ed. *Incest – Confronting the silent crime* (Minnesota Program for Victims of Sexual Assault, 1979)

NATIONAL CHILDREN'S BUREAU *Child sexual abuse and incest: a review of research* (NCB, 1982)

NATIONAL COUNCIL FOR CIVIL LIBERTIES, *Sexual Offences: Evidence to the Criminal Law Revision Committee* (NCCL Report 13, 1976)

NELSON, S. 'The kind and gentle girl who stabbed her father to death' *Irish Times* 9/4/78

'Noreen Winchester: sympathy and prejudice' *Irish Times* 10/4/78

PHILLIP, E. 'La personalitie des delinquants d'inceste' *Acta medicinae legalis et socialis, Liège*, 19 (1966)

RAEBURN, A. 'On Incest' *Cosmopolitan* (Jan. 26th, 1980)

RAPHLING, D. et al. 'Incest: a genealogical study' *Archives of General Psychiatry*, 16 (1967)

de RASCOVSKY, M. and de RASCOVSKY, A. 'On consummated incest' *International Journal of Psychoanalysis*, 31 (1950)

RENVOIZE, J. *Incest: a family pattern* (Routledge & Kegan Paul, 1982)

RHINEHART, T. 'Genesis of overt incest' *Comprehensive Psychiatry*, 2:6 (1961)

RIEMER, S. 'A research note on incest' *American Journal of Sociology*, 45 (1940)

ROSENFELD, A. et al. 'Incest and the sexual abuse of children' *Journal of American Academy of Child Psychiatry*, 16:2 (1977)

RUSH, F. 'The sexual abuse of children: a feminist point of view', in *Rape, the First Sourcebook for Women*, edited by C. Wilson and N. Connell (Plume, New American Library, New York, 1974)

RUSH, F. *The best kept secret: sexual abuse of children* (Prentice-Hall, 1980)

SCHEURELL, R. and RINDER, I. 'Social networks and deviance: a study of lower class incest, wife beating and nonsupport offenders' *Wisconsin Sociologist*, 10:2 (1973)

SCHULTZ, L. 'The child sex victim: social, psychological and legal perspectives' *Child Welfare,* 52:3 (1973)

SCOTTISH COUNCIL FOR CIVIL LIBERTIES, *Comment on Scottish Law Commission's Memorandum 44, Discussion Paper* (SCCL, 1980)

SCOTTISH LAW COMMISSION, *Memorandum 44. The law of incest in Scotland* (1980)

Scottish Law Commission, no. 69. The Law Of Incest In Scotland : Report on a reference under section 3(1)(e) of the Law Commissions Act 1965 (HMSO, Cmd 8422, 1981)

SCOTTISH WOMEN'S AID INCEST GROUP *Information pack on incest* (Women's Aid, 1983)

SEMONOVA, E. 'A study of children of incestuous matings' *Human Heredity,* 21:2 (1971)

SGROI, S. 'Sexual molestation of children: the last frontier in child abuse' *Child Today,* 4:3 (1975)

SHEFFIELD MEN AGAINST SEXUAL HARASSMENT (SMASH) *Sexual harassment, rape and sexual abuse of children: an information pack for men* (SMASH, 1983) Available from: SMASH, c/o Lifespan, Dunford Bridge, Sheffield

SLOANE, P. and KARPINSKI, E. 'Effects of incest on the participants' *American Journal of Orthopsychiatry,* 12:4 (1942)

SNOWDON, R. 'Working with incest offenders: excuses, excuses, excuses' *Aegis* 29 (autumn 1980)

STUCKER, J. 'The story of Mary C.' *Ms,* 5:10 (1977)

SUMMIT, R. and KRYSO, J. 'Sexual abuse of children: a clinical spectrum' *American Journal of Orthopsychiatry* 48 (1978)

SWEETMAN, R. *On Our Backs: Sexual Attitudes In A Changing Ireland* (Pan, 1981)

TORMES, Y. *Child Victims Of Incest* (American Humane Association, Denver, 1972)

TSAI, M. and WAGNER, N. 'Therapy groups for women sexually molested as children' *Archives of Sexual Behaviour* 7:5 (1978) 'Incest and molestation: problems of childhood sexuality' *Resident and Staff Physician* (March 1979)

VIRKUNNEN, M. 'Incest offences and alcoholism' *Medicine, Science and the Law,* 14 (1974)

'Victim-precipitated paedophilia offences' *British Journal of Criminology* 15 (April 1975)

WALKER, ALICE *The Color Purple* (The Women's Press, 1983) Fiction

WARD, E. *Father daughter Rape* (The Women's Press, 1984)

WASOFF, F. 'What is Wrong with Incest?' *SCOLAG Bulletin,* 47 (1980)

WEBER, E. 'Sexual abuse begins at home', *Ms,* 5:10 (1977)

WEEKS, R. 'The sexually exploited child' *Southern Medical Journal*, 69

WEINBERG, S. K. *Incest Behaviour* (Citadel, New York, 1955)

WEINER, I. B. 'Father–daughter incest: a clinical report' *Psychiatric Quarterly*, 36 (1962)

'On incest: a survey' *Excerpta Criminologica* (1964)

WEST, D. *Sexual victimization* (Gower, 1985)

WILL, D. 'Approaching the incestuous & sexually abusive family' *Journal of Adolescence* 6 (1983)

YORUKOGLU, A. and KEMPH, J. 'Children not severely damaged by incest with a parent' *Journal of Child Psychiatry*, 5 (1966)

ZAPHIRIS, A. *Incest: the family with two known victims* (American Humane Association, Child Protection Division, 1978)